MEATLESS DIABETIC COOKBOOK

Over 100 Easy Recipes Combining
Great Taste with Great Nutrition

BARBARA GRUNES

WITH

LINDA R. YOAKAM, M.S., R.D., L.D.
NUTRITIONAL CONSULTANT

PRIMA PUBLISHING

To my Mother and teacher, Edith Wolfe Maniff, and to my husband, Jerome Grunes, who encourages me.

PRIMA PUBLISHING and colophon are registered trademarks of Prima Communications, Inc.

A per serving nutritional breakdown is provided for each recipe. If a range is given for an ingredient amount, the breakdown is based on the smaller number. If a range is given for servings, the breakdown is based on the smaller number. If a choice of ingredients is given in an ingredient listing, the breakdown is calculated using the first choice. Nutritional content may vary depending on the specific brands or types of ingredients used. "Optional" ingredients or those for which no specific amount is stated are not included in the breakdown.

Library of Congress Cataloging-in-Publication Data

Grunes, Barbara.
    Meatless diabetic cookbook : over 100 easy recipes combining
great taste with great nutrition / Barbara Grunes.
      p. cm.
Includes index.
ISBN 0-7615-1019-2
    1. Diabetes—Diet therapy—Recipes.   2. Vegetarian cookery.
I. Title.
RC662.G726   1997
641.5′ 6314—dc21   97-19463
                                               CIP

97 98 99 00 01 HH 10 9 8 7 6 5 4 3 2 1
Printed in the United States of America

How to Order

Single copies may be ordered from Prima Publishing, P.O. Box 1260BK, Rocklin, CA 95677; telephone (916) 632-4400. Quantity discounts are also available. On your letterhead, include information concern-ing the intended use of the books and the number of books you wish to purchase.

Visit us online at www.primapublishing.com

CONTENTS

● ● ● ● ● ● ● ● ● ● ● ● ● ● ● ● ● ● ●

FOREWORD

● ● ● ● ● ● ● ● ● ● ● ● ● ● ● ● ●

A MEATLESS DIET OFFERS MANY advantages to those with diabetes and those who just want to eat a healthier diet. A meatless diet focuses on foods at the base of the Food Guide Pyramid, which the U.S. Department of Agriculture

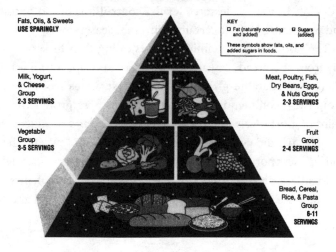

Food Guide Pyramid
A Guide to Daily Food Choices

Fats, Oils, & Sweets
USE SPARINGLY

KEY
□ Fat (naturally occurring   ▨ Sugars
and added)   (added)

These symbols show fats, oils, and
added sugars in foods.

Milk, Yogurt,
& Cheese
Group
2-3 SERVINGS

Meat, Poultry, Fish,
Dry Beans, Eggs,
& Nuts Group
2-3 SERVINGS

Vegetable
Group
3-5 SERVINGS

Fruit
Group
2-4 SERVINGS

Bread, Cereal,
Rice, & Pasta
Group
6-11
SERVINGS

● ● ● ●

v

(with the U.S. Department of Health and Human Services) developed to help consumers make healthful food choices.

The *Meatless Diabetic Cookbook* has been designed to help people with diabetes incorporate into their diets more foods from the base of the Food Guide Pyramid. Eating more beans, grains, fruits, and vegetables increases fiber intake and adds variety to the diet. Cutting out meat reduces intake of saturated fats, cholesterol, and, often, calories. More important for diabetics, sticking to a vegetarian diet ensures consumption of foods most likely to help your body control your blood glucose level, while you avoid foods that contribute to cardiovascular disease (often a side effect of diabetes).

The Food Guide Pyramid is based on the *Dietary Guidelines for Americans*, which is intended to help people develop long-term healthy eating habits. Both the pyramid and the guidelines aim to provide ample essential nutrients and encourage minimal consumption of fat, saturated fat, cholesterol, and added sugars. The foods at the base of the pyramid—breads, cereal, rice, and pasta—are excellent sources of vitamins, minerals, and fiber, and are relatively low in fat and saturated fat, and are naturally free of cholesterol. Plant foods are also rich in substances that research indicates may be beneficial in controlling blood glucose levels, reducing blood cholesterol levels, controlling blood pressure, and protecting against certain forms of disease.

The Food Guide Pyramid suggests eating 6 to 11 servings per day from the bread, cereal, rice, and pasta group; 3 to 5 servings from the vegetable group; and 2 to 4 servings from the fruit group. It recommends making food from these groups the focal point of most meals. Only 4 to 6 servings of dairy products, nuts, dried beans, and eggs are suggested. Fats, oils, and sweets (the top and smallest portion of the pyramid) should be eaten sparingly.

Meatless diets—based on beans, grain products, fruits, and vegetables—fit effectively into the Food Guide Pyramid and have a number of classifications. Vegetarian diets allow only plant products. No animal food sources are allowed, including fats and oils. With careful planning and professional assistance, strict vegetarian diets can be made to be complete in protein, calcium, vitamin B_{12}, iron, and other nutrients found in animal food sources. Lacto-ovo vegetarian diets incorporate both eggs and dairy products, which allows for a proper balance of proteins and the incorporation of calcium-rich foods. The recipes in this cookbook are based on lacto-ovo vegetarian principles: a diet primarily based on beans, grains, fruits, and vegetables that allows milk, eggs, cheese, and yogurt to improve the variety, consistency, nutritional composition, and flavor of meals.

This cookbook offers a world of food choices from the base of the Food Guide Pyramid. Carefully thought-out and planned vegetarian meals using the recipes in this book can significantly help people with diabetes and others who want to change their eating habits. After all, if a dish looks appealing and tastes just as good, *everyone* will want to try it.

Linda R. Yoakam, M.S., R.D., L.D.
Nutritional Consultant
Naperville Nutrition Network

INTRODUCTION

• • • • • • • • • • • • • • • •

THIRTY YEARS AGO, THIS COOKBOOK would not have been written. Back then, the United States was still building its own unique cuisine, borrowing heavily from many countries. Cookbook authors created recipes to emulate haute cuisine—dishes full of cream and sugar adapted from the French. The food was delicious and creative, but it wasn't necessarily good for us.

In my own family's culinary history, the rich, calorie-laden, high-salt, and high-fat foods we ate were a welcome change from the lean years of the Great Depression. I recall my childhood with loving memories, but shudder to think of all the holiday feasts, Friday-night dinners, and birthday parties that arrived like fancy floats in an endless parade for extended family. Though there was little junk food in those days, there was an unrelenting supply of roasts, lamb, chicken, pastas, vegetables, and potato dishes, all swimming in seas of gravy and cream. There were stews and soups—high in salt and glistening with fat—cookies, cakes, pies, and homemade ice cream chock-full of real butter, eggs, and cream. We ate saturated fat, sugar, and salt with reckless abandon.

Later, when I first started writing cookbooks, I carried on that grand American tradition of hearty, heavy cooking. Every member of the family was to rise from the table groaning and rubbing a full stomach. Over the years, two events—one jarring and traumatic and the other a gradual awakening—have caused a great change in my culinary philosophy. First, two of the most important people in my life became diabetic: My mother was diagnosed with diabetes at age 40, and, years later, my husband faces the illness known as non-insulin-dependent diabetes. Since then, I have focused on creating recipes that diabetics could enjoy, and I practice "medicine" through ingredients selection and food preparation. Second, in the past decade, Americans in general have become increasingly aware of nutrition and diet, and demand recipes (and restaurant meals) that use healthier ingredients and follow sensible rules of food preparation. As a cookbook author, I could not ignore this culinary revolution. I decided it was time to write a book for diabetics that was creative, interesting, and full of healthful recipes.

Before the food market's awareness of the needs of diabetics, it frustrated me to watch my mother trying to change her cooking habits without the aid of the wonderful and varied sugar-free products and lowfat foods that are now available. There was a time when I would prepare two meals: one using traditional rich recipes treasured by my family for years and another virtually identical, but substituting lowfat ingredients and using little or no sugar and interesting herbs in place of all the salt. Nondiabetic family members would often unwittingly eat from my mother's side of the serving platters—and I received nothing but compliments!

More recently, as I cook for my husband, I am sensitive to the idea that the key to his good health is what he eats. The cooking techniques and ingredients I use will help keep him healthy. Jerry has always loved sweets, particularly puddings and pies, and he always craves bread. I have, by necessity, had to create new recipes to satisfy his culinary passions and at the same time preserve his health and well-being.

It is Jerry's (and my) revelation to find that creative cooking and healthful eating are not mutually exclusive. Lowfat, low-salt, and low-calorie recipes can, and should, be every bit as tasty as the old familiar meals. And in many cases, these new healthier recipes are much simpler for the home cook to prepare.

There is no need for the diabetic to feel that he or she has to eat different foods. The purpose of this book was to create recipes that can satisfy *everyone*. All the recipes in this book have been nutritionally evaluated, including calories, percent of calories from fat, fat content, saturated fat, cholesterol, sodium, protein, sugar, and food exchanges. For your safety and peace of mind, check with your own nutritionist and doctor to see how these recipes fit into your personal, restricted diet. Then serve them to the whole family.

APPETIZERS
AND SOUPS

• • • • • • • • • • • • • • • •

• • • • • • • • • • • • • • • •

APPETIZERS AND SOUPS

APPETIZERS IS SOMETHING of a misnomer. Rather than encouraging an appetite, these dishes fend off hunger pangs—in a most diplomatic and enjoyable manner. But whatever their role, appetizers provide wonderful variety, contributing complementary and contrasting tastes to any menu.

Appetizers are always crowd-pleasers and can be so satisfying that they are often eaten as an entire meal. These tasty dishes are too often used solely for entertaining and dinner parties. Diabetics and dieters have made gargantuan displays of will-power and reluctantly avoided these small morsels, which traditionally have been rich, salty, calorie-laden delights. I have endeavored to create appetizer recipes that are irresistible to everyone. I encourage those with diabetic restrictions to try them; the days of deprivation are over.

Soups offer unlimited variety and are incredibly adaptable. A soup can be served as a pre-entrée dish, main course, luncheon, or midnight snack. Soups can be thin and delicate or robust and hearty, cooling on a hot summer day or warming in winter. This chapter features unique recipes as well as basic ones, but they are all easy to prepare with ingredients that are readily available, nourishing, healthful, and, above all, delicious.

Fresh Tomato Bruschetta

YIELD: 4 SERVINGS

For an Italian taste of tomatoes, capers, and basil, try this crunchy bruschetta.

Olive oil nonstick cooking spray
1 cup sliced red onions
¾ cup chopped ripe beefsteak tomatoes
2 tablespoons capers, rinsed and drained
½ teaspoon dried basil
½ teaspoon dried oregano
¼ teaspoon black pepper
4 cloves garlic, minced
1 teaspoon good-quality olive oil
4 slices Italian or French bread, 1 inch thick
¼ cup (1 ounce) shredded reduced-fat Monterey Jack cheese
Fresh basil leaves (optional)

SPRAY a nonstick frying pan with olive oil cooking spray; heat. Stir in onions.

Cook, partially covered for 5 minutes, stirring occasionally, or until onions are tender. Stir in chopped tomatoes, capers, basil, oregano, and pepper. Continue cooking 2 to 3 minutes or until vegetables are heated through, stirring occasionally.

Heat broiler. In a small bowl, combine garlic and oil. Brush garlic mixture over bread slices. Spoon heated tomatoes evenly over bread and sprinkle with cheese. Place bruschetta on a baking sheet. Broil in the center of the oven for about 3 minutes, until cheese melts. Garnish with fresh basil leaves. Serve hot.

NOTE: Always use fresh herbs if possible. Try growing a small herb garden, even if it's in small pots on the kitchen windowsill. Raise only the herbs that you use most frequently. Dried herbs are available year-round, but they are stronger in flavor than fresh ones and tend to lose their flavor quickly. Keep them well sealed for best results, and toss them out if you haven't used them after a year or so.

EACH SERVING PROVIDES:
143 calories, 23% calories from fat, 3.8 g fat, 1.3 g saturated fat,
5.1 mg cholesterol, 394 mg sodium, 6 g protein, 2 g sugar
FOOD EXCHANGES:
0.0 milk, 0.0 veg., 0.0 fruit, 1.5 bread, 0.0 meat, 0.5 fat

Grilled Tuscan-Style Kabobs

YIELD: 6 SERVINGS

The flavors of the vegetables used in these kabobs blend well with each other. For best results, spray the grill screen with nonstick cooking spray before grilling kabobs. This prevents individual veggies from sticking to the grill.

Kabobs
6 bamboo skewers
6 mild pickled peppers, drained
2 medium or small zucchini, cut in 1½-inch pieces
6 small pitted black olives
12 cherry tomatoes, washed and drained
Olive oil nonstick cooking spray

Italian dressing
2 tablespoons fresh lemon juice
1 tablespoon balsamic vinegar
½ teaspoon dried oregano
½ teaspoon dried basil
2 cloves garlic, minced
¼ teaspoon salt
¼ teaspoon black pepper

SOAK bamboo skewers in cold water for 20 minutes. Drain on paper towels. Thread the skewers evenly with vegetables, starting with a pickled pepper and continuing until all of the skewers have been threaded with peppers, zucchini, olives, and cherry tomatoes.

In grill, heat the coals until ashen. Lightly spray the kabobs with nonstick cooking spray. In a small bowl, combine lemon juice, vinegar, oregano, basil, garlic, salt, and pepper. Brush kabobs with dressing.

When the coals are ready, place kabobs on a sprayed grill rack about 6 inches from the heat. Grill kabobs about 4 minutes, turning once or twice as needed. Vegetables should be hot and beginning to color. Using a pot holder, transfer kabobs to a serving dish and serve hot.

EACH SERVING PROVIDES:
26 calories, 25% calories from fat, 0.9 g fat, 0.1 g saturated fat,
0 mg cholesterol, 303 mg sodium, 1 g protein, 2 g sugar
FOOD EXCHANGES:
0.0 milk, 1.0 veg., 0.0 fruit, 0.0 bread, 0.0 meat, 0.0 fat

Grilled Corn and Pepper Relish with Tarragon Biscuits

YIELD: 6 SERVINGS

This tangy relish goes great with the herbed biscuits.

3 cups hickory chips
Butter-flavored nonstick cooking spray
3 large ears corn, husks and silk removed
2 medium yellow or red bell peppers, seeds removed
    and chopped
1 cup chopped red onion
½ cup chopped cilantro or parsley
1½ tablespoons red wine vinegar
6 lettuce leaves
Tarragon Biscuits (see page 10)

COVER the hickory chips with water and soak for one hour. In grill, heat coals until ashen. Drain hickory chips and sprinkle them over the hot coals. Spray grill screen with nonstick cooking spray before setting over grill rack. Spray ears of corn with cooking spray and grill, turning every few minutes until they begin to color. Grill peppers in the same manner. When it has cooled a bit, cut corn from the cob and put it in a bowl. Stir in peppers. Add onion and cilantro, and stir in vinegar.

To serve, set a lettuce leaf on each plate and spoon relish into the center. Serve at room temperature with Tarragon Biscuits.

NOTE: For less smoke and a more intense heat when grilling, always use hardwood briquets. Try applewood chips or maple chips, or look around the garden and see what is available. For a good source of hardwood charcoal and chips contact: Peoples Smoke-N-Grill, 75 Mill St., Cumberland, RI 02864. The slightly smoky flavor gives the relish its distinctive taste.

EACH SERVING PROVIDES:
298 calories, 17% calories from fat, 6 g fat, 2 g saturated fat,
2 mg cholesterol, 483 mg sodium, 9 g protein, 6 g sugar
FOOD EXCHANGES:
0.0 milk, 0.0 veg., 0.0 fruit, 3.0 bread, 0.0 meat, 1.0 fat

Tarragon Biscuits

YIELD: 12 BISCUITS

These biscuits are light and airy with a delicate tarragon flavor.

Butter-flavored nonstick cooking spray
1 cup sifted cake flour
1 cup unbleached all-purpose flour
2½ teaspoons baking powder
Scant ½ teaspoon baking soda
½ teaspoon salt
3 tablespoons dried tarragon
2 tablespoons vegetable shortening
1¼ cups buttermilk

PREHEAT oven to 450 degrees F. Spray or grease a round 7- or 8-inch baking pan. In a large bowl, combine flours, baking powder, baking soda, salt, and tarragon. With a pastry blender, cut in shortening. Pour in just enough buttermilk to make a soft, sticky dough. With a dough scraper, gather dough together onto a floured pastry board. Flour your hands and pat dough into a ½ -inch thickness. Cut biscuits with a 2- to 2½-inch round cutter. Place the biscuits, with sides touching, in the prepared pan.

Repeat the process with the remaining scraps of dough. Bake biscuits in the center of the oven for 10 minutes, or until they are light brown on top. Serve hot.

EACH BISCUIT PROVIDES:
104 calories, 22% calories from fat, 3 g fat, 1 g saturated fat,
1 mg cholesterol, 285 mg sodium, 3 g protein, 2 g sugar
FOOD EXCHANGES:
0.0 milk, 0.0 veg., 0.0 fruit, 0.0 bread, 0.0 meat, 0.5 fat

Cherry Tomatoes Stuffed with Eggplant Purée

YIELD: 8 SERVINGS

These stuffed tomatoes are a colorful appetizer full of flavor.

1 large eggplant
1 cup chopped onion
¾ cup dried whole wheat bread crumbs
2 tablespoons nonfat plain yogurt, or to taste
3 cloves garlic, minced
½ cup chopped cilantro or parsley
1 tablespoon balsamic vinegar
¼ cup nonfat red wine salad dressing
32 cherry tomatoes

PREHEAT oven to 375 degrees F. Pierce eggplant several times with the tip of a knife or fork. Set it on a piece of aluminum foil. Bake in the center of the oven for 1 hour, or until soft. Allow eggplant to cool. Peel and chop eggplant. Mix remaining ingredients, except tomatoes, in a bowl, or process them in a food processor. Put eggplant purée in a covered container and refrigerate several hours or overnight. Stir before using.

Cut tomatoes in half, scoop out seeds, and drain upside down on a paper towel. Using a small spoon, fill each tomato with purée creating a mound on top. Set filled tomatoes on a platter and serve.

EACH SERVING PROVIDES:
109 calories, 10% calories from fat, 2.3 g fat, 0.3 g saturated fat,
0 mg cholesterol, 202 mg sodium, 4 g protein, 5 g sugar
FOOD EXCHANGES:
0.0 milk, 0.0 veg., 0.0 fruit, 1.5 bread, 0.0 meat, 0.0 fat

Asian Pancakes

YIELD: 8 SERVINGS

Asian Pancakes are similar to egg foo yung in that the vegetables are mixed in the egg batter and are served in a light sauce.

Pancake sauce
1 cup vegetable stock
1 tablespoon cornstarch
2 teaspoons lite soy sauce

Pancakes
1 egg, slightly beaten
5 egg whites
½ teaspoon salt
¼ teaspoon pepper
1 tablespoon canola oil
2 cloves garlic, minced
1 teaspoon grated fresh ginger
¾ cup minced green onions
¾ cup bean sprouts, washed and drained
¾ cup sliced mushrooms
Nonstick cooking spray

To prepare sauce, heat vegetable stock in a small saucepan over medium heat. Remove ¼ cup of the stock and whisk together with cornstarch in a small bowl. Return stock–cornstarch mixture to pot and mix well. Blend in soy sauce. Continue cooking until sauce thickens slightly. Set aside.

To prepare pancakes, beat together egg and egg whites in a deep bowl. Add salt and pepper. Set aside. In a nonstick frying pan, heat oil over medium heat. Add garlic, ginger, and onions and cook for about 1 minute, stirring often. Add bean sprouts and mushrooms and cook 1 minute. Remove from heat and stir vegetables into egg batter. Spoon 2 to 3 tablespoons of egg pancake batter into pan. With a spatula, turn pancakes when they brown on the bottom, about 2 minutes. Continue cooking until lightly brown on second side. Remove from pan and keep warm. Continue making pancakes until all of the batter has been used. Between batches, spray pan with nonstick cooking spray.

To serve, drizzle each pancake with sauce.

EACH SERVING PROVIDES:
142 calories, 17% calories from fat, 2.8 g fat, 0.4 g saturated fat,
27 mg cholesterol, 238 mg sodium, 7 g protein, 7 g sugar
FOOD EXCHANGES:
0.0 milk, 3.0 veg., 0.0 fruit, 0.0 bread, 1.0 meat, 0.5 fat

Baked Crisp Rosemary Potato Skins with Tzatziki

YIELD: 8 SERVINGS

Serve these savory potato skins with Tzatziki for the flavor of Greece. Reserve the potato innards for another recipe or serve mashed as a side dish.

4 baking potatoes, 6 to 7 ounces each, scrubbed
    and skin left on
Butter-flavored or olive oil nonstick cooking spray
2 tablespoons nonfat Italian salad dressing
1 teaspoon garlic powder
2 teaspoons crumbled dried rosemary

PREHEAT oven to 425 degrees F. Pierce potatoes several times with the tip of a small sharp knife. Bake potatoes in the center the oven for 1¼ hours, or until tender.

When potatoes are cool enough to handle, cut them into quarters, scoop out the flesh with a teaspoon, leaving ¼ inch of the flesh on the skin. Spray potato skins with cooking spray and brush lightly with salad dressing. Sprinkle with garlic powder and rosemary. Set skins on a nonstick baking sheet and return to the oven for 10 minutes, or until hot and crisp. Turn skins once.

Cut potato skins horizontally and serve hot with Tzatziki.

EACH SERVING PROVIDES:
115 calories, 4% calories from fat, 0.5 g fat, 0.2 g saturated fat,
1.5 mg cholesterol, 191 mg sodium, 7 g protein, 5 g sugar
FOOD EXCHANGES:
0.0 milk, 0.0 veg., 0.0 fruit, 1.5 bread, 0.0 meat, 0.0 fat

Tzatziki

YIELD: 8 SERVINGS

This cool, delightful cucumber and yogurt dip is also good served with warm pita bread. Its robust garlic flavor always adds flair.

Cheesecloth (about 2 feet)
3 cups nonfat plain yogurt
1 cup peeled, seeded, grated or chopped cucumber
4 cloves garlic, minced, or to taste
½ teaspoon good-quality olive oil
2 tablespoons chopped fresh dill or 1 teaspoon dill seeds
¼ teaspoon salt
¼ teaspoon white pepper

DOUBLE line a colander with cheesecloth. Set colander over a bowl. Spoon yogurt into the center of the colander. Allow yogurt to drain for 1½ to 2 hours. Discard excess yogurt liquid. Transfer yogurt into a bowl.

Add the cucumber, garlic, olive oil, dill, salt, and pepper to the yogurt and mix. Adjust seasonings to taste. Cover bowl lightly and refrigerate until ready to serve. Keeps well for a few days, covered, in refrigerator. Serve with baked potatoes, potato skins, or warm pita bread.

EACH SERVING PROVIDES:
55 calories, 8% calories from fat, 0.5 g fat, 0.1 g saturated fat,
1.5 mg cholesterol, 133 mg sodium, 5 g protein, 5 g sugar
FOOD EXCHANGES:
0.5 milk, 0.0 veg., 0.0 fruit, 0.0 bread, 0.0 meat, 0.0 fat

Grilled Portabella Open-Faced Sandwich

YIELD: 8 SERVINGS

Save the mushroom stems for soup or the stockpot.

Chive marinade
1/4 cup red wine vinegar or balsamic vinegar
1 teaspoon good-quality olive oil
2 teaspoons canola oil
1 teaspoon fructose or 2 teaspoons sugar
1/2 cup minced chives
2 teaspoons dried basil
1 teaspoon crumbled rosemary
1/4 cup vegetable stock

Sandwich
4 large whole portabella mushroom tops, scrubbed
Nonstick cooking spray
4 slices whole wheat bread or bread of your choice
1/4 cup grilled rosemary sprigs or chopped cilantro,
    for garnish

To prepare the marinade, combine vinegar, oils, fructose, chives, basil, rosemary, and stock. Mix well. Set cleaned mushroom caps facing up in a glass pie plate. Brush with marinade and drizzle remaining marinade over the mushrooms. Let them marinate for 2 hours, covered, at room temperature or overnight in the refrigerator.

In grill, heat coals until ashen. Place grill rack sprayed with nonstick cooking spray 4 to 6 inches from the heat source. Set drained mushrooms on the rack, cover grill, and grill mushrooms for 2 to 3 minutes. Turn mushrooms over using a long-handled spatula. Grill for another 2 to 3 minutes, uncovered, or until mushrooms are warm and firm to the touch but not mushy. As mushrooms are cooling, toast bread lightly on grill on both sides. Arrange toast on a plate, then set 1 mushroom on top of each slice of bread. Cut bread in half. Serve warm, decorated with rosemary sprigs or sprinkled with cilantro.

EACH SERVING PROVIDES:

73 calories, 30% calories from fat, 3 g fat, 0.3 g saturated fat, 0 mg cholesterol, 86 mg sodium, 4 g protein, 2 g sugar

FOOD EXCHANGES:

0.0 milk, 0.0 veg., 0.5 fruit, 1.5 bread, 1.0 meat, 0.0 fat

White Bean and Chick-Pea Dip with Pita Chips and Crudités

YIELD: 8 TO 10 SERVINGS

Crudités are assorted vegetables cut into pieces the perfect size for grazing. Try sliced zucchini, blanched asparagus, cherry tomatoes, sliced cucumbers, green onions, mushrooms, and colorful pepper strips.

Dip

4 cloves garlic, minced

2 cans (15 ounces each) cannellini beans, drained and rinsed

2 cups cooked drained chick-peas

⅔ cup dried basil

2½ tablespoons fresh-squeezed orange juice

1 tablespoon grated orange peel

½ teaspoon salt

¼ teaspoon pepper

⅛ teaspoon ground nutmeg

Whole wheat pita chips

4 whole wheat pita bread pockets

Butter-flavored nonstick cooking spray

4 teaspoons oregano

IN a food processor, blend garlic, beans, and chick-peas until smooth (or mash together in a bowl with a potato masher). Add basil, orange juice, orange peel, salt, pepper, and nutmeg. Spoon bean dip into a serving bowl and serve with cut vegetables and/or pita chips. Dip is best served at room temperature.

To prepare pita chips, cut each pita horizontally and then cut each half into wedges. Set pita pieces on a nonstick cookie sheet sprayed with cooking spray. Preheat oven to 350 degrees F. Spray pita chips lightly with butter-flavored cooking spray and sprinkle with oregano.

Bake in the center of the oven for 7 minutes or until bread is lightly toasted. Mound chips into a serving basket or bowl and serve immediately with room-temperature dip.

EACH SERVING PROVIDES:
252 calories, 9% calories from fat, 3 g fat, 0.2 g saturated fat,
0 mg cholesterol, 517 mg sodium, 15 g protein, 1 g sugar
FOOD EXCHANGES:
0.0 milk, 0.0 veg., 0.0 fruit, 3.5 bread, 0.0 meat, 0.0 fat

Mushroom Wontons
with Chili Sauce

YIELD: 8 SERVINGS

Perfect to include in a complete Asian meal, Mushroom Wontons can be served immediately after they are cooked or sautéed lightly and then served. Or enjoy them in soup as a dumpling. The sauce and filling can be prepared a day before serving.

Chili sauce
Olive oil nonstick cooking spray
1 teaspoon good-quality olive oil
½ cup chopped green onions
3 cloves garlic, minced
1 can (16 ounces) crushed tomatoes, including juice
1 can (4 ounces) chopped mild or spicy green chilies, drained
1 jalapeño pepper, carefully seeded and chopped
2 teaspoons chili powder
½ teaspoon oregano
¼ teaspoon salt

Mushroom wontons
1 teaspoon lowfat margarine
1 teaspoon canola oil
½ cup chopped shallots
2 cups cleaned chopped white or brown mushrooms
½ teaspoon dried marjoram
¼ teaspoon salt
¼ teaspoon pepper
24 sheets wonton wrappers
1 egg white, slightly beaten
2 tablespoons unbleached all-purpose flour to sprinkle
   on cookie sheet

To prepare sauce, spray a nonstick saucepan with olive oil cooking spray, add olive oil, and heat. Sauté onions and garlic over medium heat, adding a few tablespoons of the tomato liquid as necessary if onions begin to stick. Stir in crushed tomatoes, chilies, jalapeño pepper, chili powder, oregano, and salt. Bring mixture to a boil. Reduce heat to low and continue cooking, uncovered, for 10 to 12 minutes. Sauce will thicken slightly.

To prepare mushroom filling, heat margarine and oil in a sprayed nonstick frying pan over medium heat. Sauté shallots and mushrooms, stirring occasionally, until mushrooms are cooked and almost dry. Add marjoram, salt, and pepper. Adjust seasonings to taste. Allow filling to cool.

To assemble wontons, set 1 scant tablespoon of filling in the center of a wonton wrapper. Brush outside edge of wrapper with slightly beaten egg white. Fold wrapper in half, making a triangular shape, and press along the edges, sealing the wonton. Set wontons on lightly floured cookie sheet until they are all assembled. Cover with plastic wrap to prevent drying. Fill a medium saucepan or wok half-full with water, bring to a boil, and slide half of the wontons into the boiling water. Cook for 1½ to 2 minutes, or until the wontons are hot. Remove wontons with a slotted spoon and place in a single layer on a sprayed, heated platter. Repeat until all of the wontons are cooked.

Set 3 hot wontons on each dish and drizzle with warm chili sauce.

EACH SERVING PROVIDES:
124 calories, 15% calories from fat, 2 g fat, 0.3 g saturated fat,
3.3 mg cholesterol, 568 mg sodium, 6 g protein, 3 g sugar
FOOD EXCHANGES:
0.0 milk, 1.0 veg., 0.0 fruit, 1.0 bread, 0.0 meat, 0.5 fat

Pickled Fall Vegetables

YIELD: 8 TO 10 SERVINGS

Pickled Fall Vegetables can be prepared and kept refrigerated up to two weeks before serving. They need to marinate at least three days to taste their best.

1 cup peeled sliced cucumber
1 cup thinly sliced carrots, cut on the diagonal
1 cup thinly sliced red or yellow bell pepper
1 cup thinly sliced red onions
2 cups cauliflower florets
2½ cups white wine vinegar
1 tablespoon black peppercorns
½ cup chopped dill weed
1 teaspoon ground mustard

IN a large saucepan filled with lightly salted water, add cucumber, carrots, pepper, onions, and cauliflower. Bring water to a boil and continue cooking for 2 minutes. Drain vegetables. Put them in a glass bowl.

In a small saucepan, add vinegar, peppercorns, dill weed, and mustard. Bring pickling mixture to a boil. Remove pan from heat and pour hot liquid over vegetables making sure that the vegetables are covered with pickling mixture. Cover with plastic wrap and refrigerate for 3 days before serving. Toss vegetables once a day.

EACH SERVING PROVIDES:
4 calories, 6% calories from fat, 0.4 g fat, 0 g saturated fat,
0 mg cholesterol, 12 mg sodium, 6 g protein, 2 g sugar
FOOD EXCHANGES:
0.0 milk, 2.0 veg., 0.0 fruit, 0.0 bread, 0.0 meat, 0.0 fat

Cabbage and Tomato Soup with Fresh-Grated Ginger

YIELD: 6 SERVINGS

Make this soup when tomatoes are at their peak of flavor.

6 cups thinly sliced green cabbage
½ cup sliced onion
Nonstick cooking spray
1 can (28 ounces) chopped tomatoes, including juice
1 tablespoon fresh lemon juice
2 tablespoons brown sugar replacement
   (available at large supermarkets)
½ teaspoon salt
1 teaspoon fresh-grated ginger
¼ teaspoon pepper
1 cup water

PLACE sliced cabbage and onion in a heavy saucepan sprayed with nonstick cooking spray. Cook 5 minutes over medium heat, stirring often. Stir in tomatoes and juice, lemon juice, brown sugar replacement, salt, ginger, and pepper.

Cover and cook until vegetables are tender, about 35 minutes, stirring occasionally. Add 1 cup water, heat again, and serve.

EACH SERVING PROVIDES:
52 calories, 7% calories from fat, 0.5 g fat, 0.1 g saturated fat,
0 mg cholesterol, 408 mg sodium, 3 g protein, 7 g sugar
FOOD EXCHANGES:
0.0 milk, 2.0 veg., 0.0 fruit, 0.0 bread, 0.0 meat, 0.0 fat

Minestrone Soup

YIELD: 8 SERVINGS

This hearty Italian soup can almost be considered a meal itself.

2 teaspoons canola oil
Nonstick cooking spray
1 cup thinly sliced onion
1 cup sliced celery
1 cup sliced carrots
8 cups vegetable stock or water
1½ cups scrubbed, diced potatoes, skin left on
1½ cups sliced zucchini
1 can (15 ounces) crushed tomatoes, including liquid
1½ cups thinly sliced cabbage
¾ cup cooked white beans
¾ cup cooked macaroni
2 teaspoons dried basil
1 teaspoon dried sage
1 teaspoon salt
¼ teaspoon pepper

HEAT oil in a soup pot or other large pot sprayed with non-stick cooking spray over medium heat. Sauté onions, celery, and carrots until soft, about 5 minutes, stirring occasionally. Mix in vegetable stock, potatoes, zucchini, tomatoes and juice, and cabbage.

Bring soup to a boil, reduce heat to medium-low, partially cover, and simmer for 30 minutes. Mix in beans, macaroni, and seasonings. Adjust seasonings to taste. Simmer for 10 minutes. Serve hot.

EACH SERVING PROVIDES:
160 calories, 9% calories from fat, 1.7 g fat, 0.2 g saturated fat, 0 mg cholesterol, 458 mg sodium, 6 g protein, 4 g sugar
FOOD EXCHANGES:
0.0 milk, 0.0 veg., 0.0 fruit, 2.0 bread, 0.0 meat, 0.5 fat

Red Pepper Soup

YIELD: 6 SERVINGS

The combination of red peppers, paprika, and potatoes make this Hungarian soup rich and satisfying.

1 tablespoon canola oil
1 cup chopped onions
3 cloves garlic, minced
2½ cups seeded, sliced red bell peppers
1 tablespoon sweet paprika
1 tablespoon unbleached all-purpose flour
½ teaspoon caraway seeds
1½ cups scrubbed, diced potatoes, skin left on
1 can (15 ounces) crushed tomatoes, including liquid
6 cups vegetable stock
½ teaspoon dried marjoram
½ teaspoon salt
¼ teaspoon pepper

HEAT oil in a soup pot or other large pot. Sauté onions, garlic, and peppers over medium heat until tender, stirring occasionally. Stir in paprika, flour, and caraway seeds. Add diced potatoes, crushed tomatoes and liquid, vegetable stock, marjoram, salt, and pepper. Reduce heat to medium-low and cook, partially covered, for 40 minutes. Stir occasionally.

Serve hot. This soup is especially tasty served with a dollop of nonfat plain yogurt on top.

EACH SERVING PROVIDES:
175 calories, 15% calories from fat, 3.1 g fat, 0.3 g saturated fat,
0 mg cholesterol, 376 mg sodium, 5 g protein, 0 g sugar
FOOD EXCHANGES:
0.0 milk, 0.0 veg., 0.0 fruit, 2.0 bread, 0.0 meat, 0.5 fat

Potato–Watercress Soup

YIELD: 6 SERVINGS

This light summer soup can be served hot or cold.

2 teaspoons lowfat margarine
Butter-flavored nonstick cooking spray
2 cups sliced leeks, white part only
2 cups scrubbed, peeled, diced potatoes
6 cups vegetable stock
1 can (16 ounces) crushed tomatoes, including liquid
3 tablespoons balsamic vinegar
3 bay leaves
1 cup chopped watercress
¾ teaspoon salt
½ teaspoon pepper
½ teaspoon dried coriander

H EAT the margarine in a soup pot sprayed with cooking spray. Slowly sauté leeks and potatoes over medium heat, slowly adding 2 cups of vegetable stock. Cook until potatoes are just about tender. Do not let the leeks brown. Allow to cool, then purée vegetables. Return leek and potato purée to a clean pot.

Stir in the remaining 4 cups stock, tomatoes and liquid, vinegar, bay leaves, watercress, salt, pepper, and coriander. Reheat. Discard bay leaves. Ladle soup into individual bowls and serve hot.

EACH SERVING PROVIDES:
134 calories, 7% calories from fat, 1.1 g fat, 0.2 g saturated fat,
0 mg cholesterol, 858 mg sodium, 4 g protein, 4 g sugar
FOOD EXCHANGES:
0.0 milk, 0.0 veg., 0.0 fruit, 2.0 bread, 0.0 meat, 0.0 fat

Squash Bisque

YIELD: 8 SERVINGS

This smooth and creamy soup is perfect for company.

Soup
Butter-flavored nonstick cooking spray
½ cup minced onion
1½ tablespoons grated fresh ginger
4 cups peeled, seeded, thinly sliced butternut squash,
    about 1½ pounds
3 cups vegetable stock
¾ cup evaporated skim milk
½ teaspoon ground cinnamon
¼ teaspoon grated nutmeg
2 teaspoons brandy flavoring or 1 to 2 tablespoons brandy
½ teaspoon salt
¼ teaspoon white pepper

Garnish
2 tablespoons nonfat plain yogurt
½ cup chopped red apple

HEAT a medium-size saucepan sprayed with cooking spray over medium-low heat until hot. Add onion and ginger; stir. Cook, partially covered, until tender, 4 to 5 minutes. If onions begin to stick, add a few tablespoons of vegetable stock. Add the squash and remaining vegetable stock. Bring mixture to a boil. Reduce heat to medium-low, cover, and continue cooking until squash is tender, 15 to 20 minutes. Allow to cool, then purée.

Return squash mixture to a clean saucepan. Stir in evaporated milk, cinnamon, and nutmeg. Bring soup to boil; reduce heat to medium-low. Stir in brandy flavoring. Season with salt and white pepper.

In a small bowl, combine the yogurt and chopped apple. Serve the soup hot, garnished with a dollop of the yogurt–apple mixture.

EACH SERVING PROVIDES:

85 calories, 3% calories from fat, 0.3 g fat, 0 g saturated fat, 0.9 mg cholesterol, 333 mg sodium, 3 g protein, 6 g sugar

FOOD EXCHANGES:

0.0 milk, 0.0 veg., 0.0 fruit, 1.0 bread, 0.0 meat, 0.0 fat

Root Vegetable and Barley Soup

YIELD: 8 SERVINGS

The barley adds nourishment and the leeks, parsnips, and carrots lend a distinct flavor. It takes a little time to assemble the ingredients but the result is worth the effort.

2 teaspoons canola oil
Butter-flavored nonstick cooking spray
2 cups chopped onion
2 cups sliced leeks, white part only
1½ cups sliced carrot
2 cups sliced parsnip
2 quarts vegetable stock
2 teaspoons dried thyme
1 teaspoon salt, or to taste
1 teaspoon dried sage
½ teaspoon pepper
3 cups cooked instant barley
¼ cup chopped chives (optional)

HEAT oil in a large nonstick pot sprayed with cooking spray. Sauté onions, leeks, and carrots over medium heat, partially covered, for 5 to 6 minutes, stirring occasionally. Stir in remaining ingredients, except barley and chives. Bring soup to a boil, then reduce heat to medium-low. Continue cooking, partially covered, for 45 minutes or until all the vegetables are tender and flavors are blended. Add barley and reheat.

Adjust seasonings to taste. Ladle hot soup into bowls and sprinkle with chives.

EACH SERVING PROVIDES:
166 calories, 9% calories from fat, 2 g fat, 0.3 g saturated fat,
0 mg cholesterol, 725 mg sodium, 4 g protein, 4 g sugar
FOOD EXCHANGES:
0.0 milk, 3.0 veg., 0.0 fruit, 1.0 bread, 0.0 meat, 0.5 fat

Vegetable Stock

YIELD: ABOUT 10 CUPS

Use this broth as a base for other soups. For an even more healthful soup, leave in the vegetables or purée them and add to the broth.

3½ quarts water
2 cups sliced onions
3 potatoes, scrubbed and sliced, skins left on
½ cup sliced celery, including chopped leaves
3 tomatoes, sliced
1½ cups sliced carrots
2 cloves garlic, minced
½ cup minced parsley
1 teaspoon dried thyme
1 teaspoon dried oregano
4 bay leaves
2 teaspoons salt
¼ teaspoon fresh-ground pepper

USE a stockpot or other large pot. Place all ingredients in the pot and bring them to a boil over medium heat. Reduce heat to medium-low, cover, and continue cooking for 1½ to 2 hours, or until vegetables are well cooked.

For clear stock: Strain the cooled stock through a colander, removing vegetables. Strain the stock a second time through a finer strainer to remove any vegetable bits. You can return the reserved puréed vegetables to the soup or add fresh ones, heat, and serve. Or just use the stock in individual recipes.

Vegetable stock freezes well. For easy handling, ladle it into an ice cube tray reserved for this use only. When cubes are frozen remove them and store in a plastic bag.

EACH SERVING OF CLEAR BROTH PROVIDES:
8 calories, 6% calories from fat, 0 g fat, 0 g saturated fat,
0 mg cholesterol, 438 mg sodium, 0 g protein, 0 g sugar
FOOD EXCHANGES:
0.0 milk, 0.0 veg., 0.0 fruit, 0.0 bread, 0.0 meat, 0.0 fat

Middle Eastern Buttermilk Mint Soup

YIELD: 8 SERVINGS

A refreshing first-course or luncheon soup.

1 pound fresh spinach leaves, rinsed and chopped
1½ cups coarse cracked bulgur wheat, cooked according
   to package directions
½ teaspoon sour salt (available in the spice aisle
   of large supermarkets)
1½ cups thinly sliced green bell pepper strips
2 quarts buttermilk
½ cup chopped green onions
¾ cup chopped fresh mint or watercress

LEAVING a little water on the spinach leaves from their rinsing, place them in a nonstick saucepan, cover, and cook over medium heat for 3 to 4 minutes. Spinach will be wilted. Allow to cool.

In a deep mixing bowl, combine wheat, sour salt, bell pepper, and spinach with buttermilk, onions, and ½ cup of the mint or watercress. Chill until ready to serve.

Ladle soup into bowls and sprinkle with remaining mint or watercress.

EACH SERVING PROVIDES:
157 calories, 14% calories from fat, 2.6 g fat, 1.4 g saturated fat,
9 mg cholesterol, 438 mg sodium, 11 g protein, 13 g sugar
FOOD EXCHANGES:
1.0 milk, 2.0 veg., 0.0 fruit, 0.0 bread, 0.0 meat, 0.5 fat

SALADS

• • • • • • • • • • • • •

• • • • • • • • • • • • •

SALADS

A H, YES, THE GREENERY! To provide interesting options in this book, I have created salads that are much more than mere lettuce-based concoctions. Salads have seldom been accused of being either calorie-heavy or sugar and fat intensive. As the health-conscious know, it is the dressing and the toppings that are the villains: Bacon bits, anchovies, cheeses, croutons, and the meats, together with the rich, thick, creamy dressings added compulsively to a salad, have shot down many a diabetic's and dieter's best intentions. We seem to pay far too much lip service and far too little teeth service to salads. My motto is: Do not give away the salad, but do dump the parts that are not the salad and add healthful ingredients that make the whole dish more satisfying and tasty.

Chilled Kasha and Lentil Salad

YIELD: 6 SERVINGS

Kasha is an earthy and hearty Central European grain, while lentils are light and mild. The combination of tastes in the this salad make it appealing.

1 cup cooked kasha

1 cup cooked orange lentils

1 cup chopped green onions

1 large red bell pepper, seeded and chopped

2 cups chopped celery

3 cloves garlic, minced

1 teaspoon dried basil leaves

1 teaspoon grated lemon peel

$\frac{1}{4}$ teaspoon black pepper

3 tablespoons cider vinegar

1 teaspoon good-quality olive oil

4 cups chopped lettuce (optional)

D RAIN kasha and lentils well. Do not overcook lentils; they should be firm, not soft. Toss kasha and lentils together in a salad bowl. Mix in green onions, bell pepper, celery, garlic, basil, lemon peel, black pepper, vinegar, and olive oil. Taste to adjust seasonings. Serve on a bed of chopped lettuce.

EACH SERVING PROVIDES:
223 calories, 8% calories from fat, 2 g fat, 0.4 g saturated fat,
0 mg cholesterol, 41 mg sodium, 12 g protein, 1.6 g sugar
FOOD EXCHANGES:
0.0 milk, 0.0 veg., 0.0 fruit, 3.0 bread, 0.0 meat, 0.0 fat

Peppery Cucumber–Strawberry Salad

YIELD: 8 SERVINGS

A light, colorful salad perfect for summer.

2 cups shredded romaine lettuce
2 cups peeled, thinly sliced cucumbers
2 cups large strawberries, washed and sliced
2 teaspoons fructose or sugar
¼ teaspoon freshly ground black pepper, or to taste
¼ cup fresh lime or orange juice
2 tablespoons grated lime peel
1 tablespoon chopped fresh mint (optional)

ARRANGE lettuce on a serving plate. Arrange cucumber slices alternately with sliced strawberries decoratively on lettuce. Sprinkle strawberries and cucumbers with fructose, pepper, lime juice, lime peel, and mint. Serve chilled.

If you do not want to take the time to arrange the salad, you can toss the ingredients as you would a regular salad.

EACH SERVING PROVIDES:
24 calories, 7% calories from fat, 0.3 g fat, 0 g saturated fat,
0 mg cholesterol, 3 mg sodium, 1 g protein, 3 g sugar
FOOD EXCHANGES:
0.0 milk, 0.0 veg., 0.5 fruit, 0.0 bread, 0.0 meat, 0.0 fat

Greek Isle Salad of White Beans and Feta

YIELD: 4 SERVINGS

My oldest daughter, Reba, lives in Greece. She is my source for many Greek-based recipes, including this robust salad.

½ pound dried small white beans, soaked in water
  overnight and drained
2 cups carrots, sliced
3 bay leaves
3 cups water
4 cloves garlic, minced
1 tablespoon stoneground mustard
¼ cup fresh lemon juice
1 teaspoon good-quality olive oil
2 tablespoons oregano
½ teaspoon salt
¼ teaspoon black pepper
½ cup chopped green onions
½ cup crumbled feta cheese
½ cup chopped cilantro

IN a large pot, mix together the beans, carrots, bay leaves, and water to cover, about 3 cups. Bring mixture to a boil over high heat. Skim off any foam that may form as beans cook. Reduce heat to medium-low and continue cooking, uncovered, until beans are tender, about 2 hours. Drain. Discard bay leaves.

In a serving bowl, mix in bean–carrot mixture, garlic, mustard, lemon juice, olive oil, oregano, salt, pepper, green onions, feta cheese, and cilantro. Toss ingredients and serve at room temperature.

EACH SERVING PROVIDES:

253 calories, 13% calories from fat, 3.8 g fat, 1.5 g saturated fat,

6.3 mg cholesterol, 395 mg sodium, 15 g protein, 3 g sugar

FOOD EXCHANGES:

0.0 milk, 0.0 veg., 0.0 fruit, 3.0 bread, 1.0 meat, 0.0 fat

Spinach, Tangerine, and Couscous Salad

YIELD: 6 SERVINGS

Couscous adds body to this sweet and tangy salad.

Tangerine dressing
3 tablespoons balsamic vinegar
1 teaspoon grated tangerine or orange peel
⅓ cup fresh tangerine or orange juice
1 teaspoon dried basil
¼ teaspoon pepper

Salad
2 cups cooked couscous
2 pounds spinach, washed and cut
¾ cup diced green bell pepper
1 cup tangerine or orange slices
½ cup thinly sliced red onion

To prepare dressing, mix dressing ingredients together in a small bowl, cover, and refrigerate until ready to use. Stir before serving.

Immediately after cooking, fluff couscous with a fork and set aside in a deep bowl. For additional flavor, cook couscous in vegetable stock.

Put damp spinach in a nonstick frying pan and cover. Cook over medium heat until spinach is just wilted, about 2 minutes. Drain on paper towels. Toss spinach with couscous. Mix in bell pepper, tangerine, and red onion. Toss salad with dressing. Recipe can be prepared up to 2 to 4 hours before serving, stored in the refrigerator, and tossed again before serving.

EACH SERVING PROVIDES:
140 calories, 5% calories from fat, 0.1 g fat, 0.2 g saturated fat,
0 mg cholesterol, 126 mg sodium, 7.3 g protein, 5 g sugar
FOOD EXCHANGES:
0.0 milk, 2.0 veg., 0.0 fruit, 1.0 bread, 0.0 meat, 0.0 fat

Green Dressing
on Fresh Greens

YIELD: 6 SERVINGS

Here's a new twist: Mix yogurt with chives and parsley to create a "green on green" salad.

Green dressing
¼ cup tarragon vinegar
1 tablespoon fresh lime or lemon juice
½ cup minced chives
2 cloves garlic, mashed
1 cup nonfat plain yogurt
½ cup minced parsley or cilantro

Fresh greens
2 cups torn romaine lettuce, washed and patted dry
2 cups torn Boston lettuce, washed and patted dry
2 cups torn red leaf lettuce, iceberg lettuce, or chicory
1 cup peeled, grated beets
½ teaspoon salt
¼ teaspoon fresh-ground black pepper

To prepare the dressing, cook vinegar in a small saucepan over medium-low heat for 2 minutes. Vinegar will reduce by about half. Remove from heat and pour vinegar in a small bowl. Mix in remaining dressing ingredients.

Toss the lettuces and grated beets in a salad bowl. Season with salt and pepper. Toss salad with dressing. Serve salad on chilled plates.

EACH SERVING PROVIDES:

54 calories, 5% calories from fat, 0.4 g fat, 0 g saturated fat, 1 mg cholesterol, 244 mg sodium, 4 g protein, 5 g sugar

FOOD EXCHANGES:

0.0 milk, 2.0 veg., 0.0 fruit, 0.0 bread, 0.0 meat, 0.0 fat

Black Bean and Corn Salad

YIELD: 6 SERVINGS

Here's an easy, colorful salad that combines the soft and crunchy textures of a variety of vegetables.

2 cups cooked black beans, or 1 can (15 ounces)
  black beans, drained
2 cups cooked corn kernels, or 1 can (15 ounces)
  corn kernels, drained
½ cup chopped red onion
1 green or red bell pepper, seeded and chopped
1 cup plain nonfat yogurt
1 teaspoon cumin seeds
⅛ teaspoon pepper
4 cups torn Boston lettuce

I N a large mixing bowl, toss together black beans and corn kernels. Stir in onions and bell pepper. Add yogurt, cumin seeds, and pepper to vegetables and stir to coat. Adjust seasonings to taste.

Divide and arrange the lettuce on the salad plates. Spoon salad onto lettuce and serve.

EACH SERVING PROVIDES:
158 calories, 3% calories from fat, 0.7 g fat, 0.2 g saturated fat,
0.7 mg cholesterol, 37 mg sodium, 10 g protein, 5 g sugar
FOOD EXCHANGES:
0.0 milk, 1.0 veg., 0.0 fruit, 2.0 bread, 0.0 meat, 0.0 fat

Cabbage Salad with Lemon

YIELD: 4 SERVINGS

This crunchy salad of lemon-flavored cabbage is cholesterol-free.

3 cups thinly sliced cabbage
½ teaspoon salt
½ teaspoon celery seeds
¼ teaspoon black pepper
4 cloves garlic, minced
3 tablespoons fresh lemon juice
1 tablespoon grated lemon peel
¼ cup lowfat mayonnaise
4 tablespoons chopped fresh mint

IN a large serving bowl, toss cabbage with salt, celery seeds, and pepper. Stir in garlic, lemon juice, lemon peel, mayonnaise, and fresh mint. Cover lightly and refrigerate until serving time. Stir before serving. Garnish with extra mint leaves.

NOTE: One tablespoon of fresh herbs, such as mint, equals 1 teaspoon of dried herbs. If the fresh variety is not available or out of season use dried herbs.

EACH SERVING PROVIDES:
36 calories, 5% calories from fat, 0 g fat, 0.3 g saturated fat,
0 mg cholesterol, 468 mg sodium, 1 g protein, 3 g sugar
FOOD EXCHANGES:
0.0 milk, 1.5 veg., 0.0 fruit, 0.0 bread, 0.0 meat, 0.0 fat

EGG AND CHEESE DISHES

• • • • • • • • • • • • •

• • • • • • • • • • • • •

EGG AND CHEESE DISHES

ONE OF THE DILEMMAS in cooking for the diabetic or vegetarian is finding a pleasing substitute for the taste and texture of meat, particularly in main courses. In this chapter I have included recipes with character and taste that complement a healthful eating regimen. Too many diets limit fat, cheese, and eggs.

In these recipes I use nonfat cottage cheese, egg whites, and egg substitute, alone and in combination with real eggs to decrease the cholesterol factor. If you prefer real eggs and cheese, feel free to substitute them as you see fit.

Fall Vegetable Frittata

YIELD: 4 TO 6 SERVINGS

Serve this at brunch or luncheon. A tomato salad makes a great accompaniment.

1 tablespoon canola oil
Nonstick cooking spray
½ cup chopped shallots
3 cloves garlic, minced
2½ cups grated zucchini
½ cup thinly sliced leeks, white part only
2 teaspoons dried oregano
½ teaspoon dried rosemary
½ teaspoon salt
¼ teaspoon black pepper
¼ cup whole wheat bread crumbs
1 cup egg substitute plus 2 egg whites,
    or 4 eggs plus 2 egg whites
2 tablespoons nonfat milk

HEAT oil in a sprayed 9- or 10-inch nonstick frying pan suitable to use under the broiler. Sauté shallots and garlic for 2 to 3 minutes, stirring occasionally. Mix in zucchini and leeks. Continue cooking until vegetables are soft, about 8 minutes. Season vegetables with oregano, rosemary, salt, and pepper. Stir in bread crumbs.

Heat broiler. In a bowl, whisk together egg substitute and egg whites. Stir in milk. Spread egg mixture over vegetables. Reduce heat to medium-low. Using a spatula see that all of the vegetables are covered with the eggs, pushing any loose eggs around edges of the pan, into the vegetables. As the frittata cooks, continuously and gently lift edges of eggs with a spatula allowing them to cook. Cook 6 to 8 minutes more.

Put frying pan on center rack of the broiler for about 2 minutes, just until the eggs on top have firmed. Remove from broiler. Divide frittata evenly and serve immediately.

EACH SERVING PROVIDES:
129 calories, 28% calories from fat, 5 g fat, 1 g saturated fat,
1 mg cholesterol, 463 mg sodium, 10 g protein, 4 g sugar
FOOD EXCHANGES:
0.0 milk, 2.0 veg., 0.0 fruit, 0.0 bread, 1.0 meat, 0.5 fat

Sun–Dried Tomato Soufflé

YIELD: 4 TO 6 SERVINGS

The sun-dried tomatoes add a depth of flavor to make this soufflé extra-special. Sun-dried tomatoes are found in most well-stocked supermarkets.

Butter-flavored nonstick cooking spray
4 egg whites, at room temperature
¾ teaspoon cream of tartar
2 teaspoons reduced-calorie margarine
¾ cup chopped red onion
1 tablespoon unbleached all-purpose flour
⅓ cup evaporated nonfat milk
1½ cups chopped sun-dried tomatoes, reconstituted in
    hot water, drained, and puréed
½ cup egg substitute, or 2 eggs
½ teaspoon salt
1 teaspoon dried oregano
2 teaspoons freshly grated Parmesan or Asiago cheese

PREHEAT oven to 375 degrees F. Spray a 4-cup soufflé dish with butter-flavored nonstick cooking spray.

Beat egg whites until soft peaks form. Sprinkle in cream of tartar. Continue beating until stiff peaks form.

Spray a small nonstick frying pan with cooking spray. Heat margarine and then sauté onions until soft. Stir in flour, cooking until flour is absorbed, about 2 minutes.

In a large bowl, mix together milk, sun-dried tomato purée, egg substitute, salt, and oregano.

Fold beaten egg whites into tomato mixture. Stir in onion mixture. Lightly spoon soufflé into prepared dish. Sprinkle cheese on top of soufflé.

Bake in the center of the oven for 25 minutes. Soufflé will be puffy and golden brown, but will deflate easily, so handle gently. If it deflates, it will still taste great. Remove from oven and rush soufflé to the table to serve immediately.

EACH SERVING PROVIDES:
134 calories, 13% calories from fat, 2 g fat, 1 g saturated fat,
2 mg cholesterol, 864 mg sodium, 12 g protein, 1 g sugar
FOOD EXCHANGES:
0.0 milk, 0.0 veg., 0.0 fruit, 1.0 bread, 1.0 meat, 0.0 fat

Cheddar Pancakes with Parsnip Purée

YIELD: 6 SERVINGS (18 PANCAKES)

An elegant, savory cheese pancake served with a warm, sweet parsnip purée.

Parsnip purée
1 medium parsnip, peeled and sliced
¼ cup buttermilk
½ teaspoon powdered ginger
¼ teaspoon salt
¼ teaspoon black pepper

Cheddar pancakes
½ cup unbleached all-purpose flour
½ cup yellow or white cornmeal
2 cups buttermilk
½ teaspoon baking powder
1 tablespoon reduced-calorie margarine, softened
½ cup egg substitute plus 1 egg white,
    or 2 eggs plus 1 egg white
¼ cup (1 ounce) grated, reduced-fat Cheddar cheese
Nonstick cooking spray

To prepare parsnip purée, boil the parsnip over medium heat. Continue cooking until fork tender. Drain. Mash parsnip together with ¼ cup buttermilk, ginger, salt, and pepper. Spoon into a covered container and refrigerate until needed. Reheat to serve.

To prepare pancakes, combine flour and cornmeal in a deep bowl. Whisk in 2 cups buttermilk, baking powder, margarine, egg substitute and egg white, and cheese. Let batter stand for 20 minutes. Stir before using.

Heat a sprayed or greased nonstick frying pan. Slide pancake batter by the heaping tablespoon onto the hot frying pan. Cook pancakes until they bubble. Turn pancakes with a spatula and cook until just golden brown. Serve pancakes hot over a pool of parsnip purée.

EACH SERVING PROVIDES:

111 calories, 16% calories from fat, 3 g fat, 2 g saturated fat,

6 mg cholesterol, 349 mg sodium, 9 g protein, 5 g sugar

FOOD EXCHANGES:

0.0 milk, 0.0 veg., 0.0 fruit, 2.0 bread, 0.0 meat, 0.5 fat

Cheese and Black Bean Quesadillas with Spicy Salsa

YIELD: 4 SERVINGS

A quesadilla is a pan-fried filled tortilla. This version pairs mild cottage cheese and flavorful black beans with hot salsa.

Spicy salsa
1 cup seeded, chopped tomato
3 cloves garlic, minced
½ cup chopped red onion
⅓ cup finely chopped cilantro
2 tablespoons fresh lime juice
2 jalapeño peppers, carefully seeded and chopped, or to taste

Quesadillas
½ cup nonfat cottage cheese
4 (6-inch) flour tortillas
½ cup rinsed, drained cooked black beans, mashed
¼ cup shredded reduced-fat Monterey Jack cheese
Nonstick cooking spray

To prepare salsa, toss all of the salsa ingredients together in a bowl. To infuse flavors, cover and let stand for 45 minutes before serving. Toss salsa again before serving. You will have about 2 cups of sauce.

To prepare quesadillas, spread cottage cheese evenly over half of each tortilla. Spread beans, Jack cheese, and about ½ cup salsa over the cottage cheese. Fold quesadillas in half.

Spray a nonstick frying pan and heat pan. Cook 2 quesadillas at a time, depending on the size of the pan. Cook 3 to 4 minutes or until tortilla is a golden brown on both sides, turning once. Cut quesadillas in half. Serve hot.

NOTE: To avoid skin and eye irritation, always use rubber gloves when handling jalapeño peppers—and keep your hands away from your eyes.

EACH SERVING PROVIDES:
217 calories, 22% calories from fat, 6 g fat, 2 g saturated fat,
10 mg cholesterol, 460 mg sodium, 14 g protein, 2 g sugar
FOOD EXCHANGES:
0.0 milk, 0.0 veg., 0.0 fruit, 2.0 bread, 1.0 meat, 0.5 fat

Cottage Cheese, Grits, and Walnut Salad

YIELD: 6 SERVINGS

Horseradish and mustard add zing to the flavors of this salad.

"Salad"
2 cups medium grits, cooked
Olive oil nonstick cooking spray
1 teaspoon canola oil
2 cups white or brown sliced mushrooms
1 cup (8 ounces) nonfat cottage cheese

Horseradish dressing
2 teaspoons white horseradish
3 hard-cooked egg whites, chopped
1 teaspoon stoneground mustard
2 teaspoons tarragon vinegar
¼ cup chopped chives
¼ teaspoon salt
¼ teaspoon black pepper

Garnish
2 tablespoons chopped walnuts

PUT cooked, cooled grits in a salad bowl. Heat oil in a sprayed nonstick frying pan. Sauté mushrooms over medium heat until cooked, stirring often. Toss mushrooms with grits. Mix in cottage cheese.

Mix dressing ingredients in a small bowl. Toss dressing with "salad." Sprinkle chopped walnuts on salad and serve.

EACH SERVING PROVIDES:

166 calories, 17% calories from fat, 4 g fat, 0.3 g saturated fat,

0 mg cholesterol, 436 mg sodium, 0 g protein, 5 g sugar

FOOD EXCHANGES:

0.0 milk, 2.0 veg., 0.0 fruit, 1.0 bread, 1.0 meat, 0.0 fat

Spinach Manicotti

YIELD: 6 SERVINGS

An Italian classic, these stuffed tubes of pasta make a great party dish.

1½ cups Tomato Sauce (see page 70)
12 manicotti shells

Spinach–ricotta filling
1 package (16 ounces) light ricotta cheese
2 pounds spinach, cooked, drained, squeezed very dry, and chopped
2 teaspoons dried basil
2 egg whites
2 tablespoons freshly grated Parmesan or pecorino cheese
2 cloves garlic, minced
¼ cup chopped parsley
½ teaspoon salt
¼ teaspoon black pepper
Olive oil nonstick cooking spray

PREPARE Tomato Sauce and set aside.
Cook manicotti in boiling water according to package directions. Drain on paper towels.

To prepare filling, combine the ricotta, spinach, basil, egg whites, Parmesan cheese, garlic, parsley, salt, and pepper in a large mixing bowl. Mixture should be soft and ready to spoon into the manicotti.

Preheat oven to 350 degrees F. Spray a 9 by 13-inch nonstick baking pan with olive oil nonstick cooking spray. Spoon ¼ cup Tomato Sauce in bottom of pan. Stuff manicotti shells carefully with filling by holding one at a time in your hand and gently spooning the filling into it. Stuff each shell as full as possible without splitting the tube. Set each shell in a single layer in the pan. Spoon remaining sauce over stuffed manicotti.

Cover with aluminum foil and bake in the center of the oven for 25 to 30 minutes. Uncover and continue baking for 5 to 6 minutes.

To serve, arrange 2 manicotti shells on each plate. Serve immediately.

EACH SERVING PROVIDES:
328 calories, 14% calories from fat, 5 g fat, 0.1 g saturated fat, 13 mg cholesterol, 758 mg sodium, 21 g protein, 5 g sugar
FOOD EXCHANGES:
0.0 milk, 2.0 veg., 0.0 fruit, 3.0 bread, 1.0 meat, 0.5 fat

Spinach Lasagna

YIELD: 6 SERVINGS

Another Italian classic, lasagna is always a family favorite.

3 cups Tomato Sauce (see page 70)
6 ounces cholesterol-free lasagna noodles,
  cooked and drained
2 cups nonfat cottage cheese
¾ cup (about 6 ounces) fresh spinach, stems discarded,
  washed, and patted dry

SPREAD 1 cup Tomato Sauce over the bottom of a 6 by 9-inch baking pan. Arrange half of the noodles over sauce and spread half of the cottage cheese on top of the noodles. Arrange half of the spinach on top of cottage cheese. Repeat layering. Pan will be very full, but it will cook down during baking. Cover pan with aluminum foil.

Preheat oven to 350 degrees F. Bake lasagna in the center of the oven for 30 minutes. Remove pan from oven and gently press any exposed noodles into sauce. Return it to oven and continue baking for 15 minutes. Let stand for 5 minutes before serving.

EACH SERVING PROVIDES:
250 calories, 8% calories from fat, 3 g fat, 1 g saturated fat,
0 mg cholesterol, 903 mg sodium, 17 g protein, 6 g sugar
FOOD EXCHANGES:
0.0 milk, 2.0 veg., 0.0 fruit, 2.0 bread, 1.0 meat, 0.0 fat

Egg and Cheese Dishes
••••

Easy Pan-Fried
Cheese Ravioli

YIELD: 6 SERVINGS

This quick dish is delicious as an entrée or an appetizer. Pan-frying the pasta adds a delicious crispness.

Cowpoke Barbecue Sauce (see page 68) or
    Yellow Pepper Sauce (see page 69)
2 packages (9 ounces each) refrigerated lowfat cheese ravioli
Butter-flavored nonstick cooking spray
1 ½ cups sliced green onions

COOK ravioli according to package directions. Drain in a single layer on paper towels.

Heat a sprayed nonstick frying pan. Sauté green onions and ravioli until ravioli are lightly brown on each side, turning once.

Divide ravioli and onions onto individual plates, drizzle with Cowpoke Barbecue Sauce (page 68) or Yellow Pepper Sauce (page 69) and serve hot.

EACH SERVING PROVIDES:
260 calories, 8% calories from fat, 3 g fat, 1 g saturated fat,
5 mg cholesterol, 639 mg sodium, 16 g protein, 3 g sugar
FOOD EXCHANGES:
0.0 milk, 0.0 veg., 0.0 fruit, 1.0 bread, 0.0 meat, 0.5 fat

Raspberry Blintzes

YIELD: 6 SERVINGS

These crepes, stuffed with a slightly sweet cheese mixture and topped with a raspberry-orange sauce, are a good choice for a special meal. Traditionally, blintzes are served with a spoonful of sour cream, but you could substitute plain nonfat yogurt if desired.

Crepes
½ cup egg substitute, or 2 eggs
1 cup unbleached all-purpose flour
½ teaspoon salt
1 cup water
Butter-flavored nonstick cooking spray

Cheese filling
2 cups nonfat cottage cheese
1 egg white
1 tablespoon fructose, or 2 tablespoons sugar
2 tablespoons grated orange peel
2 tablespoons fresh-squeezed orange juice
1 cup fresh raspberries, blackberries, or other berries, washed and drained

Raspberry sauce
1½ cups fresh raspberries, washed
3 tablespoons fresh-squeezed orange juice
1 teaspoon fructose, or 2 teaspoons sugar

CREPES can be prepared the day before serving. In a mixing bowl or blender, mix together egg substitute, flour, salt, and water. Scrape down sides of the bowl with a rubber spatula as necessary. Before cooking batter, let it stand, covered, for 20 minutes. Stir before using.

Use a nonstick crepe pan. It is only necessary to spray it with cooking spray for the first and second crepes. Warm prepared pan over medium-high heat. Use a ¼ cup measuring cup and pour in batter for each crepe. Working quickly, lift and tilt the pan to evenly distribute batter. Cook crepe until bottom is golden brown. Turn and cook only a few seconds more. Remove and stack crepes with a sheet of aluminum foil between them. Repeat until all of the crepes are cooked. Either fill immediately or cover crepes and refrigerate until ready to use.

To prepare filling, purée the cottage cheese in a blender or food processor. Add remaining filling ingredients and blend. Set aside.

To prepare sauce, combine sauce ingredients in a small saucepan and simmer over medium heat for 5 minutes, stirring often. Remove from heat and pour into a serving bowl. Cool. Refrigerate until ready to serve. You will have about 1½ cups sauce.

To assemble, use 12 crepes, reserving remaining crepes for another day (they freeze well). Spread about 2 tablespoons of the filling in the center of each crepe. Fold over, envelope style: bottom first, then sides, and fold down the top. Turn over so sealed side is on the bottom.

Heat a sprayed a nonstick frying pan over medium heat. Fry blintzes seam side down until golden brown on both sides. Put 2 blintzes on each plate and drizzle sauce on top.

EACH SERVING PROVIDES:
172 calories, 2% calories from fat, 1 g fat, 0 g saturated fat,
0 mg cholesterol, 422 mg sodium, 15 g protein, 7 g sugar
FOOD EXCHANGES:
0.0 milk, 0.0 veg., 0.5 fruit, 1.5 bread, 1.0 meat, 0.0 fat

Egg and Cheese Dishes
••••

Cowpoke Barbecue Sauce

YIELD: 6 SERVINGS (1 CUP)

The slight sweetness of the brown sugar substitute, the tang of the Worcestershire sauce, and the kick of the jalapeño pepper and chili powder make this a lively accompaniment for many recipes.

Nonstick cooking spray
½ cup minced green onion
½ cup chopped green bell pepper
½ cup water
⅓ cup catsup
1 tablespoon chili powder
1 teaspoon ground cumin
2½ tablespoons red wine vinegar
2 teaspoons Worcestershire sauce
1 tablespoon brown sugar substitute
1 jalapeño pepper, carefully seeded and chopped

HEAT a sprayed nonstick saucepan. Sauté onion and bell pepper over medium heat for 2 to 3 minutes, stirring often. Stir in water and remaining ingredients. Simmer for 5 minutes. Cool and transfer to a serving bowl. Cover and refrigerate until ready to serve. Stir before serving.

EACH SERVING PROVIDES:
32 calories, 10% calories from fat, 1 g fat, 0 g saturated fat,
0 mg cholesterol, 222 mg sodium, 1 g protein, 3 g sugar
FOOD EXCHANGES:
0.0 milk, 0.0 veg., 0.0 fruit, 0.5 bread, 0.0 meat, 0.0 fat

Yellow Pepper Sauce

YIELD: 4 TO 6 SERVINGS

Green or red bell peppers can be substituted for the yellow peppers, but the yellow sauce is a snazzy alternative to an ordinary sauce. It is tasty and light in character.

2 large yellow bell peppers
2 cloves garlic, minced
2 tablespoons white wine
1 teaspoon good-quality olive oil
Salt and white pepper to taste

REMOVE tops and seeds from peppers and cut in pieces. Cook all ingredients in a sprayed, covered saucepan for 5 to 8 minutes, stirring often and checking to make sure there is enough liquid. If not, add more water or wine by the tablespoon as needed.

Transfer sauce to a covered container and refrigerate until needed. Stir before serving. The sauce is best served hot.

EACH SERVING PROVIDES:
53 calories, 23% calories from fat, 2 g fat, 0.2 g saturated fat,
0 mg cholesterol, 0.4 mg sodium, 2 g protein, 0 g sugar
FOOD EXCHANGES:
0.0 milk, 2.0 veg., 0.0 fruit, 0.0 bread, 0.0 meat, 0.0 fat

Tomato Sauce

YIELD: 6 SERVINGS (1½ CUPS)

Not only is this sauce quick and easy, it's versatile, too.

1 teaspoon olive oil
Olive oil nonstick cooking spray
4 cloves garlic, minced
1 cup chopped onions
1 can (16 ounces) crushed tomatoes, including juice
⅓ cup tomato sauce
3 tablespoons tomato paste
2 teaspoons dried basil
2 teaspoons dried oregano
¼ teaspoon salt
⅛ teaspoon black pepper

HEAT olive oil in a sprayed nonstick frying pan. Sauté garlic and onion for about 5 minutes, stirring occasionally. Stir in crushed tomatoes, tomato sauce, tomato paste, basil, oregano, salt, and pepper. Reduce heat to medium-low. Continue cooking, uncovered, for 12 to 15 minutes.

Stir occasionally. Sauce will thicken as it cooks.

EACH SERVING PROVIDES:
50 calories, 19% calories from fat, 1.2 g fat, 0.2 g saturated fat,
0 mg cholesterol, 10 mg sodium, 2 g protein, 3 g sugar
FOOD EXCHANGES:
0.0 milk, 2.0 veg., 0.0 fruit, 0.0 bread, 0.0 meat, 0.0 fat

VEGETABLES
AND BEANS

VEGETABLES AND BEANS

*A*LWAYS A REFRESHING PART of any meal, vegetables have begun to take center stage in many diets. With the growth of farmer's markets and interest in fresh, locally grown produce, the availability of fresh vegetables has increased. Clever cooks take advantage of the very first sweet corn and juicy vine-ripened red and yellow tomatoes of summer. Spring brings asparagus and fresh peas, just to name a couple of that season's treats.

You'll find bean recipes everywhere in this book—not just in this chapter. Beans show up in soups, salads, and main dishes—everywhere but desserts. Diabetics and vegetarians know that beans are an important source of protein; they are also rich in calcium, phosphorus, and iron. Beans make an excellent substitute for meat. They satisfy our need for diverse flavors and fill us up.

There is another more practical and realistic advantage that beans have over meat: the difference in cost. Once you start using beans in place of meat, you will find that you can include items on your grocery list that you might have considered extravagant before. Don't hesitate to serve these dishes to everyone in your family and all your guests.

Savoy Cabbage with Couscous

YIELD: 6 SERVINGS

Savoy cabbage is a curly, bright green cabbage. Combined with couscous, it can be served as a fast and tasty side or main dish. For a change of pace, brown rice or other grains can be used in place of the couscous.

2 cups uncooked couscous or cooked brown rice
1 tablespoon good-quality olive oil
6 cups thinly cut savoy cabbage
½ cup vegetable stock or water
½ teaspoon salt
½ cup chopped dill
1 teaspoon dill seeds
½ teaspoon dried sage
¼ teaspoon black pepper

To cook couscous, bring 1¼ cups of water or vegetable stock to a boil, add 1 cup couscous, and cover. Remove from heat. Let stand for 5 minutes. Uncover and fluff couscous with a fork to separate grains.

Heat olive oil in a nonstick saucepan over medium heat. Stir in cabbage. Cover and cook for 8 to 10 minutes, stirring occasionally. The cabbage will soften almost immediately. Add vegetable stock, cooked couscous or brown rice, salt, dill, dill seeds, sage, and pepper. Stir, heat, and serve.

EACH SERVING PROVIDES:

165 calories, 20% calories from fat, 3.8 g fat, 0.5 g saturated fat, 0 mg cholesterol, 312 mg sodium, 1 g protein, 3 g sugar

FOOD EXCHANGES:

0.0 milk, 1.0 veg., 0.0 fruit, 1.5 bread, 0.0 meat, 0.5 fat

Baked Potatoes with Ricotta and Parmesan Cheese

YIELD: 4 SERVINGS

Like most good peasant food, this recipe could not be easier or tastier and is sure to please anyone who enjoys simple food. The ricotta cheese topping is cool and creamy.

4 baking potatoes, about 4 ounces each, skin left on
    and scrubbed clean
1 teaspoon good-quality olive oil
Nonstick cooking spray
3 cloves garlic, minced
¾ cup chopped green onions
3 cups fresh spinach, washed and chopped
½ cup nonfat ricotta cheese
½ teaspoon black pepper
¼ teaspoon ground nutmeg
2 tablespoons nonfat Parmesan cheese

PREHEAT oven to 425 degrees F. Pierce potatoes several times with the tip of a sharp knife or fork. Bake potatoes on a non-stick cookie sheet on the center rack of oven for 50 minutes to 1 hour, or until done. Baked potatoes are done when the tip of a knife inserted in the center of potato will slide in easily, or when the potato gives slightly when gently squeezed.

Meanwhile, prepare the topping. Heat olive oil in a sprayed nonstick frying pan. Add garlic and green onions, and sauté, partially covered, until onions are soft, stirring occasionally. Stir in spinach and continue cooking, stirring occasionally, until spinach is limp. Stir in ricotta, pepper, and nutmeg. Remove from heat.

Cut hot baked potatoes in half horizontally and gently squeeze each half open. Place half potatoes on individual dishes and spoon spinach filling over top. Sprinkle with Parmesan cheese. Serve hot.

EACH SERVING PROVIDES:
222 calories, 6% calories from fat, 2 g fat, 1 g saturated fat,
0 mg cholesterol, 84 mg sodium, 11 g protein, 1 g sugar
FOOD EXCHANGES:
0.0 milk, 0.0 veg., 0.0 fruit, 3.0 bread, 0.0 meat, 0.0 fat

Roasted Ratatouille over Herbed Polenta

YIELD: 4 SERVINGS

Ratatouille is a French country-style dish that melds together the flavors of eggplant, zucchini, tomatoes, and peppers. Serving it over the Herbed Polenta makes for a full meal and an international delight.

Olive oil nonstick cooking spray
1 cup thinly sliced onions
3 cloves garlic, peeled and minced
3 cups peeled, diced eggplant
2 cups horizontally sliced zucchini
2 cups sliced red or green bell peppers
3 cups chopped tomatoes, including any juice
2 teaspoons dried oregano
¼ cup nonfat olive oil and vinegar dressing
Salt and black pepper
Herbed Polenta (see page 110)

S PRAY an ovenproof casserole with nonstick cooking spray and preheat oven to 375 degrees F.

Add all vegetables to casserole and toss. Sprinkle with oregano, olive oil and vinegar dressing, and salt and pepper to taste.

Bake covered casserole in the center of the oven for 20 minutes. Uncover, stir vegetables, and continue baking for 25 to 30 minutes or until vegetables are tender but not too soft. Stir vegetables and ladle over warm slices of Herbed Polenta. The ratatouille is good served hot or at room temperature. It can be re-covered and refrigerated to serve a day or two later.

EACH SERVING PROVIDES:
390 calories, 14% calories from fat, 7 g fat, 1 g saturated fat,
0 mg cholesterol, 521 mg sodium, 11 g protein, 9 g sugar
FOOD EXCHANGES:
0.0 milk, 4.0 veg., 0.0 fruit, 3.5 bread, 0.0 meat, 1.0 fat

Roasted Elephant Garlic Cloves

YIELD: 4 SERVINGS OF 1 GARLIC CLOVE PER PERSON, OR ABOUT ½ CUP COOKED GARLIC, DEPENDING ON THE SIZE OF THE CLOVES

When roasted, giant garlic cloves become mild and aromatic, with almost a hint of sweetness. Squeeze cooked garlic gently out of its casing and use it over pizza crust, polenta, or mixed into a salad.

1 head elephant garlic, separated but cloves left unpeeled

PREHEAT oven to 425 degrees F. Wrap garlic loosely in a single layer of aluminum foil and place on center rack in oven. Bake garlic 1 hour or until cloves are soft when pierced with the tip of a sharp knife. Cool slightly so it can be handled. Discard foil. Cut off tops of cloves and squeeze garlic on uncooked pizza crust, cooked vegetables, or anything that suits you. Garlic with be soft and paste-like and will spread easily.

If you prefer, you can roast garlic cloves separately or in a loosened intact head.

EACH SERVING PROVIDES:
27 calories, 3% calories from fat, 0 g fat, 0 g saturated fat,
0 mg cholesterol, 3 mg sodium, 1 g protein, 0 g sugar
FOOD EXCHANGES:
0.0 milk, 1.0 veg., 0.0 fruit, 0.0 bread, 0.0 meat, 0.0 fat

Norwegian Potato Cakes

YIELD: 6 SERVINGS

This recipe for rolled potato pancakes was given to me by a friend in Iowa. They are a traditional favorite at Christmastime.

3 cups cold mashed potatoes
1 cup unbleached flour
½ teaspoon salt
1½ tablespoons reduced-calorie margarine

IN a deep bowl, mix together potatoes, flour, salt, and margarine. Divide mixture in half. On a lightly floured pastry cloth or board roll dough out to between ¼ and ⅛ inch thick. Cut pancakes into 3-inch rounds.

Heat a nonstick frying pan and cook pancakes on the hot pan until golden brown, turning only once, about 1 minute on each side.

Hot pancakes can be served "savory" with Yogurt Dill Sauce (see page 82) or "sweet" with a sprinkling of brown sugar substitute.

EACH SERVING PROVIDES:
170 calories, 12% calories from fat, 3 g fat, 1 g saturated fat,
2 mg cholesterol, 529 mg sodium, 4 g protein, 5 g sugar
FOOD EXCHANGES:
0.0 milk, 0.0 veg., 0.0 fruit, 2.0 bread, 0.0 meat, 0.5 fat

Yogurt Dill Sauce

YIELD: 8 SERVINGS (ABOUT 1½ CUPS)

Yogurt is a valuable ingredient in preparing lowfat sauces. Here dill adds its special flavor for a refreshing sauce.

1 cup plain nonfat yogurt
½ cup nonfat mayonnaise
2 cloves garlic, minced
⅓ cup snipped fresh dill, or 2 teaspoons dill seeds
¼ teaspoon white pepper

IN a small bowl, mix together the yogurt and mayonnaise with garlic, dill, and pepper. Adjust seasonings to taste. Cover and store Yogurt Dill Sauce in the refrigerator. Stir before serving.

EACH SERVING PROVIDES:
29 calories, 2% calories from fat, 0 g fat, 0 g saturated fat,
1 mg cholesterol, 212 mg sodium, 2 g protein, 2 g sugar
FOOD EXCHANGES:
0.0 milk, 0.0 veg., 0.0 fruit, 0.5 bread, 0.0 meat, 0.0 fat

Yellow Split Peas and Peppers

YIELD: 4 SERVINGS

You can serve this colorful dish hot or cold, as an appetizer or as a side dish. Pass warm pita bread with the cooked peas and peppers.

1 teaspoon good-quality olive oil
Olive oil nonstick cooking spray
4 cloves garlic, minced
2 cups sliced yellow, red, or green bell peppers
1 cup yellow split peas
3 cups water
½ teaspoon salt
3 tablespoons red wine vinegar
¼ teaspoon black pepper

HEAT olive oil in a sprayed nonstick frying pan. Sauté half of the garlic and all the bell peppers over medium heat until tender, about 5 minutes. Stir occasionally. Set aside.

In a large saucepan, cover peas with 3 cups water. Add salt and remaining garlic and stir. Cook peas over medium heat for 45 minutes; drain. Peas should be firm, not mushy. In a large bowl, combine peas, cooked peppers, vinegar, and black pepper. Adjust seasonings to taste.

EACH SERVING PROVIDES:
209 calories, 8% calories from fat, 2 g fat, 0.3 g saturated fat, 0 mg cholesterol, 276 mg sodium, 13 g protein, 4 g sugar
FOOD EXCHANGES:
0.0 milk, 0.0 veg., 0.0 fruit, 2.5 bread, 0.0 meat, 0.5 fat

Lentil–Sunflower Seed Burgers

YIELD: 6 SERVINGS

These satisfying burgers are easy to make and are perfect for a main dinner course or a fast and healthful lunch.

2 cups water
1 cup lentils, rinsed
1 cup cooked brown or white rice
¼ cup sunflower seeds
1 cup chopped green onion
1¾ cups dried whole wheat bread crumbs
⅓ cup nonfat plain yogurt
2 teaspoons stoneground mustard
½ teaspoon salt
¼ teaspoon pepper
Olive oil nonstick cooking spray
6 lettuce leaves
12 slices tomato

BOIL 2 cups water and add rinsed lentils. Reduce heat to medium-low, cover, and continue cooking for 10 minutes, or until tender but not mushy. Drain. In a large bowl, mix together cooled lentils and cooked rice. This can be done the morning of or day before serving.

To prepare the burgers, add sunflower seeds, green onions, bread crumbs, yogurt, mustard, salt, and pepper to lentil mixture; mix. Shape mixture into 6 burgers of equal size. Set them on a plate, cover lightly, and refrigerate for 1 hour.

Heat a sprayed nonstick frying pan. Cook burgers over medium heat, turning once, until they are cooked through and browned on both sides. Serve burgers in an onion bun or half of a warm pita pocket with Yogurt Dill Sauce (see page 82), lettuce, and sliced tomato.

EACH SERVING PROVIDES:
302 calories, 16% calories from fat, 5.4 g fat, 1 g saturated fat, 0 mg cholesterol, 485 mg sodium, 15 g protein, 2 g sugar
FOOD EXCHANGES:
0.0 milk, 0.0 veg., 0.0 fruit, 3.5 bread, 0.0 meat, 1.0 fat

Mushroom Crepe Pie

YIELD: 8 SERVINGS

For a variation, sauté a thinly sliced portabella mushroom and spread on top of the crepe pie at serving time.

Crepes
½ cup egg substitute, or 2 eggs
¾ cup unbleached all-purpose flour
¼ teaspoon salt
⅓ cup wheat germ
1¼ cups nonfat milk
Butter-flavored nonstick cooking spray

Filling
1 teaspoon reduced-calorie margarine
1 teaspoon canola oil
Butter-flavored nonstick cooking spray
4 cups minced mushrooms
2 cups minced shallots
1 vegetable or mushroom bouillon cube, crumbled
¼ teaspoon salt
¼ teaspoon black pepper
1 package (10 ounces) fresh spinach, washed and cut
1 cup nonfat plain yogurt

Garnish
2 tablespoons minced chives
¼ cup minced parsley or cilantro

IN a mixing bowl or blender, mix together egg substitute, flour, salt, wheat germ, and milk. Scrape down sides of the bowl with a rubber spatula as necessary. Before using batter let it stand, covered, for 20 minutes. Stir before cooking.

Heat a sprayed nonstick crepe pan over medium-high heat. It is only necessary to spray for the first and second crepes unless crepes stick to pan. In that case, spray before cooking each crepe. Use a ¼ cup measuring cup to measure and pour batter for each crepe. Lift and tilt the pan to spread the batter evenly. Turn crepe and cook only a few seconds more. Remove from heat. Repeat until all of the crepes are cooked. Crepes can be prepared the day before using. Cover each crepe with a sheet of foil and wrap them well. Refrigerate until ready to serve.

To prepare the filling, heat the margarine and oil in a sprayed nonstick frying pan. Sauté mushrooms and shallots until tender, about 3 minutes. Add bouillon, salt, pepper, and spinach and cover. Cook covered for 4 minutes, stirring occasionally. Allow to cool slightly. Blend in yogurt.

To assemble crepe pie, lay 1 crepe on a serving plate and spread with a thin layer of the cooled mushroom mixture. Top with another crepe. Continue until you have used 14 crepes. Sprinkle with chives and parsley and any remaining filling.

Cut the crepe pie with a pie server. Serve warm or at room temperature.

EACH SERVING PROVIDES:
150 calories, 11% calories from fat, 2 g fat, 0.4 g saturated fat,
1 mg cholesterol, 358 mg sodium, 10 g protein, 6 g sugar
FOOD EXCHANGES:
0.0 milk, 2.0 veg., 0.0 fruit, 1.0 bread, 0.0 meat, 0.5 fat

Spiced Cauliflower, Tomatoes, and String Beans

YIELD: 8 SERVINGS

For something a bit different, serve these vegetables seasoned with coriander, cumin, and tumeric, which give them an international flavor.

Olive oil nonstick cooking spray
½ teaspoon cumin seeds
2 teaspoons grated fresh ginger
4 cloves garlic, minced
1 small head cauliflower, washed and broken into florets
2 cups chopped tomatoes
1 cup French or regular string beans, trimmed and cut
¼ cup vegetable stock or water
¾ teaspoon ground coriander
½ teaspoon turmeric
⅛ teaspoon ground red pepper
¼ teaspoon salt

HEAT a sprayed nonstick frying pan over medium heat. Add cumin seeds. Cook until seeds are brown and begin to pop. Add ginger and garlic. Cook until soft and golden, 1 to 2 minutes. Add the cauliflower and cook until lightly browned, about 5 minutes. Stir in tomatoes, string beans, vegetable stock, coriander, turmeric, red pepper, and salt. Reduce heat to low. Cover and cook until cauliflower is tender, about 8 minutes.

Spoon hot cooked vegetables into a serving bowl and serve.

EACH SERVING PROVIDES:

40 calories, 10% calories from fat, 0.5 g fat, 0 g saturated fat,

0 mg cholesterol, 145 mg sodium, 4 g protein, 5 g sugar

FOOD EXCHANGES:

0.0 milk, 2.0 veg., 0.0 fruit, 0.0 bread, 0.0 meat, 0.0 fat

Southwest-Style Bean Salad

YIELD: 8 SERVINGS

For a change from the usual salad, try this combination of crunchy tortillas, Southwest spices, and cooked beans.

1 teaspoon good-quality olive oil
Olive oil nonstick cooking spray
2 cloves garlic, minced
2 corn tortillas, torn in pieces
½ cup Spicy Salsa (see page 58)
2 tablespoons fresh lime juice
1 teaspoon ground cumin
¼ teaspoon salt
4 cups romaine lettuce, washed, dried, and torn
1 can (15 ounces) kidney beans, drained
1 cup cooked, well drained black beans
¾ cup thinly sliced red onion
1 cup chopped green or red bell pepper
1 cup chopped tomato
½ cup chopped cilantro

HEAT olive oil in a sprayed nonstick saucepan. Sauté garlic briefly. In the same pan, fry tortilla pieces until warm. Remove from pan and set aside. In same pan, stir in salsa, lime juice, cumin, and salt. Cook for 1 minute, stirring often, just long enough to warm the sauce.

Meanwhile, in a salad bowl combine lettuce, beans, onion, bell pepper, and tomato. Add fried tortilla chips. Toss salad with warm salsa mixture. Sprinkle with cilantro and serve.

EACH SERVING PROVIDES:
126 calories, 10% calories from fat, 1.6 g fat, 0.2 g saturated fat,
0 mg cholesterol, 189 mg sodium, 8 g protein, 1 g sugar
FOOD EXCHANGES:
0.0 milk, 0.0 veg., 0.0 fruit, 1.0 bread, 1.0 meat, 0.0 fat

Spinach, Mushrooms, and Chick-Peas

YIELD: 4 TO 6 SERVINGS

If you add an additional 1½ cups of cooked hot barley or brown rice to the vegetables before serving, this vegetable dish turns into an interesting, hearty entrée.

2 teaspoons good-quality olive oil, divided
Olive oil nonstick cooking spray
3 cups sliced white mushrooms
¼ teaspoon salt
¼ teaspoon black pepper
¾ cup diced tomato, including any juice
5 ounces fresh trimmed spinach, washed but not drained
1 tablespoon red wine vinegar
1 cup cooked, drained chick-peas

HEAT 1 teaspoon of the olive oil in a sprayed nonstick frying pan. Sauté mushrooms over medium heat, until tender, about 5 minutes, stirring occasionally. Season with salt and pepper. Stir in tomatoes and spinach. Continue cooking until spinach has softened but not wilted. Splash with red wine vinegar and remaining 1 teaspoon of olive oil and stir. Stir in chick-peas and heat. Serve hot.

EACH SERVING PROVIDES:
118 calories, 27% calories from fat, 9 g fat, 0.5 g saturated fat,
0 mg cholesterol, 170 mg sodium, 6 g protein, 3 g sugar
FOOD EXCHANGES:
0.0 milk, 0.0 veg., 0.0 fruit, 0.0 bread, 0.0 meat, 0.5 fat

Greek-Style Fresh Fennel with White Beans

YIELD: 4 TO 6 SERVINGS

The mild beans combined with the licorice flavor of the fennel create a bright, fresh dish for any season.

2 teaspoons good-quality olive oil, divided
Olive oil nonstick cooking spray
½ cup chopped shallots
1 cup cooked, diced potato
1½ cups chopped green or red bell pepper
2 cups thinly sliced fennel (about 1 large bulb)
⅓ cup vegetable stock
3 cups cooked small white beans
¼ teaspoon salt
¼ teaspoon black pepper
1 tablespoon balsamic vinegar
½ cup snipped fresh dill

HEAT 1 teaspoon of the olive oil in a sprayed nonstick frying pan over medium heat. Sauté shallots until tender, about 2 minutes. Stir in potato, bell pepper, fennel, and vegetable stock. Cook until fennel is tender, stirring occasionally.

Stir in beans. Cook until hot. Season with salt, pepper, vinegar, remaining 1 teaspoon of olive oil, and fresh dill. Serve hot.

EACH SERVING PROVIDES:
318 calories, 8% calories from fat, 3.1 g fat, 0.5 g saturated fat,
0 mg cholesterol, 186 mg sodium, 16 g protein, 3 g sugar
FOOD EXCHANGES:
0.0 milk, 2.0 veg., 0.0 fruit, 0.0 bread, 0.5 meat, 0.5 fat

Baby Lima Bean Stew

YIELD: 4 SERVINGS

In this Greek vegetable dish, the flavors marry together to create a delightful, rich taste.

1 cup baby lima beans, washed and picked over
3 cups water
1½ cups sliced onions
1 cup sliced carrots
¾ cup sliced celery
3 bay leaves
⅛ teaspoon red pepper flakes
2 cups chopped tomatoes, including any liquid
2 tablespoons tomato paste
2 cloves garlic, minced
2 teaspoons dried oregano
½ teaspoon salt
¼ teaspoon black pepper
2 teaspoons balsamic vinegar
2 teaspoons good-quality olive oil

In a large saucepan, combine lima beans and 3 cups water. Cover pot and bring to a boil. Boil for 20 minutes. Stir in onions, carrots, celery, bay leaves, and red pepper flakes. Reduce heat to medium-low and cook for 1 hour. At any time during cooking, if more water is needed add it ¼ cup at a time.

Stir in tomatoes, tomato paste, garlic, oregano, salt, and pepper. Adjust seasonings to taste. Continue cooking until beans are tender but not mushy. Stir in vinegar and olive oil. If stew becomes too dry, add a small amount of tomato juice as needed. Discard bay leaves before serving. Serve as a side dish or entrée— it's delicious hot or cold.

GRAINS

• • • • • • • • • • • • • • • • •

• • • • • • • • • • • • • • • • •

GRAINS

G RAINS—SUCH AS RICE, barley, couscous, buckwheat, and oatmeal—are flexible and healthful foods that are frequently overlooked in cookbooks and menu planning. Grains can stand admirably by themselves as satisfying side or main dishes, and they can be combined easily and naturally with vegetables or pastas to make a splendid entrée. Use grains to fill out leftover dishes, sprinkle them on salads, or heat them to serve as breakfast foods.

Grains as common as millet and rice or as exotic as quinoa and amaranth are widely available in supermarkets as well as in specialty food stores. Because they are high in protein and carbohydrates, they are important additions or complements to the diabetic and vegetarian diet.

Cracked Wheat–Stuffed Grilled Green Peppers

YIELD: 6 SERVINGS

Hearty cracked wheat is good in salads and pilafs. Here it is stuffed in colorful peppers. Any extra filling can be reheated and used as a side dish at another meal.

½ cup cracked wheat
3 green or red bell peppers
1 teaspoon olive oil
Olive oil nonstick cooking spray
1 cup chopped onions
3 cloves garlic, minced
½ cup grated carrots
¼ cup currants
3 tablespoons lightly toasted sunflower seeds
½ teaspoon ground cinnamon

To cook cracked wheat, bring 1¼ cups of salted water to a boil. Stir in cracked wheat. Reduce heat to medium-low, cover, and cook for 15 to 20 minutes, until tender. Stir occasionally. Makes 1½ cups cooked cracked wheat.

Cut tops off bell peppers. Slice peppers in half horizontally and seed. Peppers can be grilled outdoors, under the broiler, on a stovetop grill, or pan-fried. With all methods, rotate peppers to brown them evenly. If you are broiling them, place skin side up; if you are grilling them, place skin side down. Using a long handled-fork, put cooked peppers into a plastic bag and seal; steam peppers for 20 minutes. Remove peppers from bag and peel by rubbing off blackened skin. Set aside.

Heat oil in a sprayed nonstick frying pan. Over medium heat, sauté onions and garlic until softened, stirring occasionally. If onions stick to pan, add a few tablespoons of water or vegetable stock. Stir in cooked cracked wheat, carrots, currants, sunflower seeds, and cinnamon. Mix until combined.

Heat oven to 350 degrees F. Spray nonstick ovenproof pan. Stuff pepper halves with filling and bake in prepared pan for 15 to 20 minutes, or until heated through. Serve hot.

EACH SERVING PROVIDES:

100 calories, 3.3% calories from fat, 27 g fat, 0.4 g saturated fat,

0 mg cholesterol, 8 mg sodium, 4 g protein, 3 g sugar

FOOD EXCHANGES:

0.0 milk, 0.0 veg., 0.0 fruit, 1.0 bread, 0.0 meat, 0.6 fat

Fried Brown Rice

YIELD: 6 SERVINGS

This recipe seems to work better using defrosted, cooked rice rather than freshly cooked rice. Cook the rice, store it in freezer containers, and freeze. When you are ready to make Fried Brown Rice, defrost rice.

1 tablespoon canola oil
1 cup finely chopped green onions
3 cloves garlic, minced
3 cups frozen cooked brown rice, defrosted
½ cup grated carrot
2 cups bean sprouts, washed and drained
¾ teaspoon salt
¼ teaspoon black pepper
2 egg whites, slightly beaten

IN a nonstick frying pan or wok, heat oil over medium heat. Sauté onions, garlic, and brown rice for 1 to 2 minutes, stir-frying (stirring often) as the food cooks. Add carrots, bean sprouts, salt, and pepper. Add beaten egg whites and stir-fry 2 minutes more, or until the eggs have set.

Working quickly, spoon the fried rice into a shallow bowl and serve hot. Or, let the rice cool, refrigerate, and serve as a cold rice salad.

EACH SERVING PROVIDES:
154 calories, 19% calories from fat, 3.3 g fat, 0.4 g saturated fat,
0 mg cholesterol, 296 mg sodium, 6 g protein, 4 g sugar
FOOD EXCHANGES:
0.0 milk, 0.0 veg., 0.0 fruit, 2.0 bread, 0.0 meat, 0.5 fat

Brown Rice and Red Bean Salad with Corn Salsa

YIELD: 4 TO 6 SERVINGS

Brown rice is minimally processed—the tough hull has been removed and the outer bran remains, making it more nutritious than white rice. Here brown rice is served with a delicious combination of beans and salsa.

1½ teaspoons canola oil
½ cup diced red onion
3 cloves garlic, minced
¾ cup sliced celery
3 cups cooked brown rice
1 cup cooked red beans, drained
½ teaspoon chili powder
¼ teaspoon cumin powder
¼ teaspoon black pepper
Corn Salsa (see page 104)

HEAT oil in a nonstick frying pan over medium heat. Stir in onion, garlic, and celery. Sauté for about 4 minutes, stirring occasionally, until vegetables are soft. Stir in rice and cook until flavors mix, 3 to 4 minutes. Add red beans, chili powder, cumin, and pepper. Adjust seasonings to taste.

Serve hot in a deep bowl with Corn Salsa on the side.

EACH SERVING PROVIDES:
300 calories, 11% calories from fat, 3.8 g fat, 0.1 g saturated fat,
0 mg cholesterol, 208 mg sodium, 11 g protein, 4 g sugar
FOOD EXCHANGES:
0.0 milk, 0.0 veg., 0.0 fruit, 4.0 bread, 0.0 meat, 0.5 fat

Corn Salsa

YIELD: 4 SERVINGS

This easy-to-prepare salsa celebrates the flavors of Mexico.

1¼ cups peeled, chopped ripe tomatoes
½ cup minced onion
¾ cup drained corn kernels
½ cup chopped cilantro
2 jalapeño peppers, seeded and chopped, or to taste
¼ teaspoon salt

IN a small bowl, combine tomatoes, onion, corn kernels, cilantro, jalapeño peppers, and salt. Cover bowl lightly and refrigerate until needed. Toss salsa again and adjust seasonings to taste before serving.

EACH SERVING PROVIDES:
50 calories, 5% calories from fat, 0.4 g fat, 0.1 g saturated fat,
0 mg cholesterol, 176 mg sodium, 2 g protein, 3 g sugar
FOOD EXCHANGES:
0.0 milk, 2.0 veg., 0.0 fruit, 0.0 bread, 0.0 meat, 0.0 fat

Barley, Pasta, and Mushrooms

YIELD: 8 SERVINGS

For a hearty balanced meal, try this old-world recipe. The pasta lightens an otherwise heavy dish.

1 teaspoon reduced-calorie margarine
Butter-flavored nonstick cooking spray
3 cloves garlic, minced
1 cup chopped onion
2 cups sliced brown or white mushrooms
6 ounces whole wheat spaghetti or other pasta
   of your choice, cooked according to package directions
   and drained
2 cups cooked instant barley
½ teaspoon salt
¼ teaspoon black pepper

HEAT margarine in a sprayed nonstick frying pan. Sauté garlic and onion over medium heat until tender, stirring occasionally. If onion begins to stick, add 3 to 4 tablespoons of water or vegetable stock. Add mushrooms and cook until mushrooms are tender, 4 to 5 minutes. Stir in pasta and cooked barley. Season with salt and pepper. Serve hot.

EACH SERVING PROVIDES:
244 calories, 6% calories from fat, 1.7 g fat, 0.4 g saturated fat,
0 mg cholesterol, 148 mg sodium, 10 g protein, 2 g sugar
FOOD EXCHANGES:
0.0 milk, 1.0 veg., 0.0 fruit, 3.0 bread, 0.0 meat, 0.0 fat

Kasha-Stuffed Cabbage Rolls

YIELD: 6 TO 12 SERVINGS (12 ROLLS)

I remember my mother lovingly making this dish for us. It is a satisfying and interesting entrée.

1 cup medium-grain roasted buckwheat (kasha), uncooked
2 egg whites, slightly beaten
2 cups water or vegetable stock

1 teaspoon canola oil
Nonstick cooking spray
1 cup chopped onions
2 cups chopped mushrooms
½ teaspoon salt
¼ teaspoon black pepper

1 medium head cabbage, outer leaves removed, cored,
    and leaves loosened
1 cup sliced onions
1 cup water
2 cups tomato juice
3 tablespoons brown sugar substitute
1 lemon, sliced thin

To cook kasha, heat 1 cup of buckwheat in a sprayed nonstick frying pan. Stir in egg whites and use a fork to coat grains as kasha cooks. Cook about 1 minute until egg whites are absorbed. Meanwhile, in a medium saucepan, bring 2 cups water or vegetable stock to a boil. Stir in kasha. Cover and return to a boil. Simmer 8 to 10 minutes, or until buckwheat is tender and liquid is absorbed. Allow to cool. Makes about 4 cups.

To prepare filling, heat oil in a sprayed nonstick frying pan over medium heat. Sauté onions and mushrooms until tender, 4 to 5 minutes, stirring occasionally. Stir in salt, pepper, and cooled kasha. Set aside.

Put cabbage in a pot with 1 inch of water on the bottom, cover, and steam until leaves are just tender but not mushy. Allow to cool and separate leaves.

Arrange onion slices on the bottom of a Dutch oven. To fill cabbage leaves, spread leaves flat, one at a time, stem side towards you, and spoon 2½ to 3 tablespoons of filling at bottom end of each leaf. Roll up cabbage leaves with filling inside and fold ends like an envelope. Place rolls in Dutch oven, in a double layer, making about 12 stuffed cabbage rolls. Add 1 cup of water and 1 cup of the tomato juice to the pan. Bring to a boil and cover. Reduce heat to medium-low and cook for 1 hour.

Preheat oven to 350 degrees F. Cool cabbage rolls slightly. Using a slotted spoon, transfer rolls from Dutch oven to a sprayed nonstick 9 by 13-inch baking pan. Sprinkle with remaining tomato juice, brown sugar substitute, and lemon slices. Bake in center of oven, uncovered, for 45 minutes. Serve hot. Any leftover stuffing can be heated and served as a side dish.

EACH SERVING PROVIDES:
106 calories, 8% calories from fat, 1.1 g fat, 0.2 g saturated fat,
0 mg cholesterol, 254 mg sodium, 5 g protein, 7 g sugar
FOOD EXCHANGES:
0.0 milk, 1.0 veg., 0.0 fruit, 1.0 bread, 0.0 meat, 0.0 fat

Grilled White Polenta with Red Peppers and Rosemary

YIELD: 8 SERVINGS

An upscale version of a classic Italian polenta dish.

1 teaspoon reduced-calorie margarine
Olive oil nonstick cooking spray
½ cup minced chives
1 cup chopped red peppers
1 quart cold water
1 cup white or yellow stoneground cornmeal
1 tablespoon chopped fresh rosemary
½ teaspoon salt
¼ teaspoon white pepper
4 teaspoons freshly grated Parmesan, Asiago,
   or Romano cheese
½ cup sliced red or green bell peppers, for garnish

HEAT margarine in a sprayed medium nonstick saucepan. Sauté chives and red peppers for about 2 minutes, stirring once or twice. Whisk cornmeal into the cold water and add the rosemary, salt, and pepper. Add cornmeal mixture to the pan with chives and peppers. Bring to a boil. Continue cooking and whisking until mixture thickens, 10 to 15 minutes.

Pour polenta into a sprayed nonstick 9-inch round cake pan. Allow to cool. Refrigerate for 20 to 30 minutes, or until polenta is firm. The polenta can be prepared the day before serving.

Cut polenta into 8 pie-shaped wedges. Spray a grill rack and heat the grill. When the coals are hot and ashen, put sprayed grill rack 4 to 6 inches from heat source. Set polenta wedges on prepared rack and grill for about 2 minutes on each side, turning once with a long-handled spatula, until hot and lightly browned.

Transfer polenta to individual serving dishes. Sprinkle with cheese and sliced bell peppers. Serve hot as a first course.

EACH SERVING PROVIDES:

97 calories, 15% calories from fat, 1.7 g fat, 0.5 g saturated fat, 2 mg cholesterol, 218 mg sodium, 3 g protein, 0 g sugar

FOOD EXCHANGES:

0.0 milk, 0.0 veg., 0.0 fruit, 1.5 bread, 0.0 meat, 0.0 fat

Herbed Polenta

YIELD: 6 SERVINGS

Polenta is a versatile food that pairs well with many flavors.

1 cup cold water
2 cups white or yellow cornmeal
2 cups boiling water
1 teaspoon sugar
1 tablespoon margarine or butter
1 tablespoon dried oregano
1 teaspoon dried basil
½ teaspoon salt
¼ teaspoon black pepper

POUR cold water into a saucepan. Using a whisk, mix in cornmeal. Add boiling water, sugar, margarine, oregano, basil, salt, and pepper. Continue cooking, whisking often, until mixture pulls away from the sides of the pan, 6 to 10 minutes. (To prevent lumpiness during cooking, always use cold water at the start and whisk the cornmeal into the water.)

Spray or grease an 8½ by 4½-inch loaf pan. Spoon polenta into the loaf pan. Smooth top with back of a spoon. Cover with aluminum foil or plastic wrap and refrigerate until polenta is firm, about 30 minutes.

Unmold the firm polenta and cut it into ½-inch strips. Either grill polenta using a sprayed grill screen on an indoor grill or spray a nonstick frying pan and sauté the polenta slices just until golden on each side.

Serve polenta warm with roasted vegetables, such as Roasted Ratatouille (page 78), on top.

EACH SERVING PROVIDES:

190 calories, 17% calories from fat, 3.5 g fat, 1 g saturated fat, 0 mg cholesterol, 214 mg sodium, 4 g protein, 2 g sugar

FOOD EXCHANGES:

0.0 milk, 0.0 veg., 0.0 fruit, 2.0 bread, 0.0 meat, 0.5 fat

Quinoa Pancakes

YIELD: 8 SERVINGS (ABOUT 24 PANCAKES)

Protein-rich, versatile quinoa flour is relatively new to American stores, but it is actually a very old grain. It was used by the ancient Incas and still is important in South American cuisine. Quinoa Pancakes are good plain, but you can serve them with sugar-free fruit syrup, too.

⅓ cup quinoa flour
1½ cups unbleached all-purpose flour
1 teaspoon sugar
2 cups finely chopped or grated ripe pear
1½ teaspoons baking powder
½ teaspoon baking soda
¼ cup egg substitute, or 1 egg, slightly beaten
2 teaspoons canola oil
1½ cups nonfat milk
¼ teaspoon ground cinnamon
1 teaspoon reduced-calorie margarine
Butter-flavored nonstick cooking spray

I N a mixing bowl, combine flours, sugar, pear, baking powder, and baking soda. Stir in egg substitute, oil, milk, and cinnamon. Let batter stand for 20 minutes. Stir.

Heat margarine in a sprayed nonstick frying pan. Pour in batter, about 3 tablespoons at a time. Cook until bubbles form and pancakes are brown on the bottom, 3 to 4 minutes. Turn pancakes gently and cook until other side is golden brown. Serve hot.

EACH SERVING PROVIDES:

177 calories, 11% calories from fat, 2.2 g fat, 0 g saturated fat, 1 mg cholesterol, 185 mg sodium, 6 g protein, 9 g sugar

FOOD EXCHANGES:

0.0 milk, 0.0 veg., 0.5 fruit, 1.5 bread, 0.0 meat, 0.5 fat

Buckwheat Pancakes with Dried Cherries

YIELD: 8 SERVINGS (ABOUT 24 PANCAKES)

These pancakes are tasty served plain, but you can also pass around some sugar-free syrup if desired.

¾ cup buckwheat flour
¼ cup unbleached all-purpose flour
1 teaspoon sugar
½ teaspoon baking soda
¼ teaspoon baking powder
¼ teaspoon salt
⅓ cup dried cherries or raisins
1½ cups buttermilk
1½ teaspoons canola oil
1 teaspoon reduced-calorie margarine
Butter-flavored nonstick cooking spray

In a mixing bowl, combine flours, sugar, baking soda, baking powder, salt, and dried cherries or raisins. Mix in buttermilk and oil. Let batter stand for 20 minutes. Stir. Heat margarine in a sprayed nonstick frying pan. Pour in batter about 2 to 3 tablespoons at a time. Cook until bubbles form and pancakes are brown on the bottom, 3 to 4 minutes. Turn pancakes gently and cook until other side is golden brown. If batter becomes too thick, add water by the tablespoon until it returns to the desired consistency. Serve pancakes hot.

EACH SERVING PROVIDES:

103 calories, 17% calories from fat, 2 g fat, 0 g saturated fat,

2 mg cholesterol, 212 mg sodium, 4 g protein, 3 g sugar

FOOD EXCHANGES:

0.0 milk, 0.0 veg., 0.0 fruit, 1.0 bread, 0.0 meat, 0.5 fat

Oatmeal with Grape-Nuts Cereal

YIELD: 3 SERVINGS

An all-time favorite comfort food is hot oatmeal for breakfast. This version adds a few special touches for a great start to the morning.

1½ cups water
¼ teaspoon salt
1½ cups steel-cut oatmeal
1 teaspoon reduced-calorie margarine
¼ teaspoon ground cinnamon
3 tablespoons Grape-Nuts cereal
Brown sugar substitute, fructose, or sugar
¼ cup raisins or dried cranberries
1 cup nonfat milk

I N a saucepan, bring water and salt to a boil. Stir in oatmeal and continue stirring as oatmeal absorbs water, 2 to 3 minutes. Stir in margarine, cinnamon, and Grape-Nuts.

Ladle hot oatmeal into bowls. Serve hot with brown sugar substitute, if desired, raisins or cranberries, and nonfat milk.

EACH SERVING PROVIDES:
253 calories, 12% calories from fat, 3.5 g fat, 1 g saturated fat,
1.4 mg cholesterol, 282 mg sodium, 11 g protein, 13 g sugar
FOOD EXCHANGES:
0.0 milk, 0.0 veg., 0.0 fruit, 3.0 bread, 0.0 meat, 0.5 fat

PIZZA AND PASTA

PIZZA AND PASTA

I T IS A RARE SOUL that does not crave pizza. I am a firm
believer in and a vocal advocate of the principle that neither
diabetics nor health-conscious people need to give up eating pizza. It takes only a little modification and imagination to
adjust most recipes. For example, the pizza crusts in this
chapter—Herbed, White Corn with Hot Red Pepper Flakes,
and Whole Wheat Fennel—are unique, delicious, and won't
violate your dietary restrictions. The pizza recipes have been
designed to meet dietary guidelines for the diabetic and yet fully
satisfy everyone's hankering for pizza.

Another favorite food, pasta, is everywhere today—from restau-
rants that serve exclusively pasta to entire cookbooks devoted
to the dish. While spaghetti has long been a standard in the
American kitchen, such pastas as conchiglie, trafalle, and
fusilli—better known as shells, bow-ties, and spirals—can now
be found in kitchen cabinets. You will find an astounding variety
of dried and fresh pastas in most supermarkets.

Pasta is equally superb served hot, warm, or cold, and its relatively quick and easy preparation makes it a joy for both the
home cook and the hungry troops.

For pasta dishes that feature cheese fillings, see the recipes for
Spinach Manicotti (page 62), Spinach Lasagna (page 64), and
Easy Pan-Fried Cheese Ravioli (page 65).

Herbed Pizza Crust

YIELD: 8 SERVINGS

Adding basil and oregano to the dough creates a flavorful, fragrant crust.

¾ cup warm water, about 110 degrees F
½ teaspoon sugar
1 package (2¼ teaspoons) active dry yeast
1½ cups bread flour
2 tablespoons dried basil
2 tablespoons dried oregano
1 tablespoon good-quality olive oil
Nonstick cooking spray

IN a small bowl, combine warm water and sugar. Stir in yeast. Place bowl in a warm, draft-free place until yeast begins to bubble. In a mixing bowl or food processor, stir together flour, basil, oregano, and olive oil. Add yeast mixture and process or mix by hand to form a somewhat sticky dough. Place dough on a lightly floured surface and knead a few minutes until a soft dough forms.

Put dough in a bowl, cover with a warm, damp kitchen towel or plastic wrap, and let stand for 1 hour. Punch dough down and let stand for 5 minutes.

Spray a 12- to 14-inch pizza pan with nonstick cooking spray and pat and roll dough into pan. At this point you can wrap crust in plastic wrap and freeze for later use or continue recipe with pizza preparation.

NOTE: You can prepare pizza crust in an electric mixer using a dough hook, in a food processor with a steel blade, or in a bowl with a wooden spoon. It will take about 3 minutes in an electric mixer, 6 to 9 seconds in a food processor, and about 6 minutes by hand. For a thinner crust (and fewer calories), you can divide the dough in half and roll each half into a 12-inch pan.

EACH SERVING PROVIDES:
115 calories, 16% calories from fat, 2.1 g fat, 0.3 g saturated fat,
0 mg cholesterol, 2 mg sodium, 4 g protein, 1 g sugar
FOOD EXCHANGES:
0.0 milk, 0.0 veg., 0.0 fruit, 1.5 bread, 0.0 meat, 0.5 fat

White Corn Pizza Crust with Hot Red Pepper Flakes

YIELD: 8 SERVINGS

The addition of cornmeal and pepper flakes to the dough gives the crust extra body and a burst of spicy flavor.

¾ cup warm water, about 110 degrees F
½ teaspoon sugar
1 package (2¼ teaspoons) active dry yeast
1 cup bread flour
½ cup white or yellow cornmeal
¼ teaspoon red pepper flakes, or to taste
1 tablespoon good-quality olive oil
Olive oil nonstick cooking spray

IN a small bowl, combine warm water and sugar. Stir in yeast. Place bowl in a warm, draft-free place until yeast begins to bubble. In a mixing bowl or food processor, stir together flour, cornmeal, red pepper flakes, and olive oil with a wooden spoon. Stir in yeast mixture. Process or mix by hand to form a somewhat sticky dough. Place dough on a lightly floured surface and knead a few minutes until a soft dough forms.

Put dough in a bowl, cover with a warm, damp kitchen towel or plastic wrap, and let stand for 1 hour. Punch dough down and let stand for 5 minutes.

Spray a 12- to 14-inch pizza pan with nonstick cooking spray and pat and roll dough into pan. To shape dough, press with a cookie sheet and again pat and roll dough into desired shape. At this point you can wrap crust in plastic wrap and freeze for later use or continue recipe with pizza preparation.

EACH SERVING PROVIDES:

106 calories, 18% calories from fat, 2.2 g fat, 0.3 g saturated fat, 0 mg cholesterol, 4 mg sodium, 3 g protein, 1 g sugar

FOOD EXCHANGES:

0.0 milk, 0.0 veg., 0.0 fruit, 1.5 bread, 0.0 meat, 0.5 fat

Whole Wheat Fennel Pizza Crust

YIELD: 8 SERVINGS

Whole wheat and the slight licorice flavor of fennel team together to make a flavorful crust with character.

¾ cup warm water, about 110 degrees F
½ teaspoon sugar
1 package (2¼ teaspoons) active dry yeast
1 cup bread flour
½ cup whole wheat flour
2 tablespoons fennel seeds
½ teaspoon fennel powder
1 tablespoon good-quality olive oil
Olive oil nonstick cooking spray

IN a small bowl, combine warm water and sugar. Stir in yeast. Place bowl in a warm, draft-free place until yeast begins to bubble. In a mixing bowl or food processor, stir together flours, fennel seeds, fennel powder, and olive oil. Stir in yeast mixture. Process to form a somewhat sticky dough. Place dough on a lightly floured surface and knead a few minutes until a soft dough forms.

Put dough in a bowl, cover with a warm, damp kitchen towel or plastic wrap, and let stand for 1 hour. Punch dough down and let stand for 5 minutes.

Spray a 12- to 14-inch pizza pan with nonstick cooking spray and pat and roll dough into pan. At this point you can wrap crust in plastic wrap and freeze for later use or continue recipe with pizza preparation.

EACH SERVING PROVIDES:

109 calories, 18% calories from fat, 2.3 g fat, 0.3 g saturated fat, 0 mg cholesterol, 3 mg sodium, 4 g protein, 1 g sugar

FOOD EXCHANGES:

0.0 milk, 0.0 veg., 0.0 fruit, 1.5 bread, 0.0 meat, 0.5 fat

Roasted Garlic and Tomato Pizza

YIELD: 6 SERVINGS

This pizza is especially good served with a crisp green salad.

1 Herbed Pizza Crust (see page 120)
Olive oil nonstick cooking spray
1 cup Roasted Elephant Garlic, about 6 cloves (see page 80)
1 large beefsteak tomato, thinly sliced
2 cups asparagus tips and pieces, cooked crisp-tender
3½ ounces goat cheese, crumbled

STRETCH and roll pizza dough into a 12-inch circle. Spray pizza dough with cooking spray.

Preheat oven to 425 degrees F. If you are using a pizza tile, set it on the lowest rack in the oven.

Spread soft roasted garlic over crust. Arrange tomatoes decoratively over the garlic. Asparagus should be cooked just until tender, with some crunch remaining. Sprinkle asparagus and crumbled goat cheese on top. Set pizza on tile or directly on center rack in oven. Bake until crust is firm and lightly golden around edges, 20 to 25 minutes. Cut pizza into 12 wedges and serve hot.

EACH SERVING PROVIDES:
223 calories, 26% calories from fat, 7 g fat, 2.9 g saturated fat,
7.6 mg cholesterol, 67 mg sodium, 10 g protein, 3 g sugar
FOOD EXCHANGES:
0.0 milk, 0.0 veg., 0.0 fruit, 2.0 bread, 0.5 meat, 1.0 fat

White Corn Pizza with Rustic Tomato Sauce and Cheese

YIELD: 6 SERVINGS

The combination of tomato sauce, cheese, and rosemary is delicious in its simplicity.

1 White Corn Pizza Crust (see page 122)
Olive oil nonstick cooking spray
1 cup Rustic Tomato Sauce (see page 130)
¼ pound lowfat or regular mozzarella cheese, shredded
   (1 cup)
¼ cup grated Romano or Parmesan cheese
½ teaspoon dried rosemary

STRETCH and roll pizza dough into a 12-inch circle. Spray pizza dough with nonstick cooking spray.

Preheat oven to 425 degrees F. If you are using a pizza tile, set it on the lowest rack in the oven.

Spread tomato sauce over crust. Sprinkle cheeses and rosemary over the sauce. Set pizza on tile or directly on center rack in oven. Bake until crust is firm and lightly golden, 20 to 25 minutes. Cut pizza into 12 wedges and serve hot.

EACH SERVING PROVIDES:
236 calories, 27% calories from fat, 7 g fat, 3.3 g saturated fat,
0 mg cholesterol, 282 mg sodium, 12 g protein, 3 g sugar
FOOD EXCHANGES:
0.0 milk, 1.0 veg., 0.0 fruit, 1.5 bread, 1.0 meat, 1.0 fat

Whole Wheat Fennel Pizza with Mushrooms

YIELD: 6 SERVINGS

Use a variety of mushrooms to make a very special pizza.

1 Whole Wheat Fennel Pizza Crust (see page 124)
Olive oil nonstick cooking spray
2 teaspoons good-quality olive oil
3 cloves garlic, minced
2½ cups sliced white mushrooms
2½ cups sliced portabella or other mushrooms
1 teaspoon dried basil
¼ teaspoon black pepper
2 cups Rustic Tomato Sauce (see page 130)

STRETCH and roll pizza dough into a 12- or 14-inch circle. Spray pizza dough with olive oil cooking spray.
Preheat oven to 425 degrees F. If you are using a pizza tile, set it on the lowest rack in the oven.

Heat oil in a sprayed nonstick frying pan. Stir in garlic and mushrooms. Cook over medium heat, partially covered, until mushrooms are tender, 4 to 5 minutes, stirring occasionally. If mushrooms begin to stick to pan, add water or vegetable stock by the tablespoon. Stir in basil and pepper. Allow to cool.

Spread tomato sauce over crust. Top with cooked mushrooms. Set pizza on tile or directly on center rack in oven. Bake 20 to 25 minutes, or until the crust is firm. Cut pizza into 12 wedges and serve hot.

EACH SERVING PROVIDES:

221 calories, 20% calories from fat, 5.2 g fat, 0.7 g saturated fat, 0 mg cholesterol, 176 mg sodium, 9 g protein, 6 g sugar

FOOD EXCHANGES:

0.0 milk, 3.0 veg., 0.0 fruit, 1.5 bread, 0.0 meat, 1.0 fat

Rustic Tomato Sauce

YIELD: 12 SERVINGS (ABOUT 3½ CUPS)

This sauce is perfect for both pasta and pizza. It can be stored in a plastic container in the refrigerator for up to 1 week, or frozen for up to 3 weeks.

Olive oil nonstick cooking spray
¼ cup water
4 cloves garlic, minced
1¼ cups thinly sliced onions
½ cup sliced celery
10 Italian plum tomatoes, or 1 can (28 ounces)
    crushed tomatoes, including liquid
1 can (6 ounces) tomato paste
2 teaspoons dried basil
2 teaspoons dried oregano
½ teaspoon dried marjoram
¼ teaspoon salt
¼ teaspoon red pepper flakes

Spray a nonstick saucepan and warm pan over medium heat. Add water, garlic, onions, celery, and tomatoes. Cook for 2 minutes. Stir in tomato paste, basil, oregano, marjoram, salt, and red pepper flakes.

Bring sauce to a boil. Reduce heat to medium-low and simmer, uncovered, for 25 minutes, stirring occasionally. Sauce will thicken as it cooks. Remove sauce from heat. Use sauce immediately or cool and place in a covered container and store in the refrigerator.

Ten-Minute Spaghetti Sauce over Orzo

YIELD: 6 SERVINGS

Use only good-quality olive oil for this recipe.

2 teaspoons olive oil
1 cup chopped onions
4 cloves garlic, minced
½ cup grated carrot
1 cup sliced green or red bell peppers
1 cup sliced or grated zucchini
¼ to ⅓ cup water or vegetable stock
1 can (28 ounces) crushed tomatoes, including juice
2 teaspoons oregano
3 bay leaves
½ teaspoon salt
¼ teaspoon black pepper
12 ounces uncooked orzo pasta

HEAT olive oil in a nonstick saucepan over medium heat. Sauté onions, garlic, carrot, bell peppers, and zucchini partially covered until tender, stirring occasionally. If vegetables begin to stick, add ¼ to ⅓ cup water or vegetable stock. Stir in tomatoes and juice, oregano, bay leaves, salt, and pepper. Bring sauce to a boil, reduce heat to medium low, and continue cooking for 10 minutes.

While sauce is cooking, boil orzo until just tender. Drain.

Divide orzo onto 6 plates, top with hot spaghetti sauce, and serve.

EACH SERVING PROVIDES:

329 calories, 9% calories from fat, 3.3 g fat, 0.5 g saturated fat,

0 mg cholesterol, 400 mg sodium, 11 g protein, 7 g sugar

FOOD EXCHANGES:

0.0 milk, 3.0 veg., 0.0 fruit, 3.0 bread, 0.0 meat, 0.5 fat

Sun-Dried Tomato Pesto

YIELD: 16 SERVINGS

Sun-dried Tomato Pesto is a deep and flavorful sauce made without cooking. The tomatoes are available dried or preserved in olive oil. To reduce calories, use the dried tomatoes (not packed in oil) and reconstitute them in boiling water.

2 firmly packed cups yellow or red sun-dried tomatoes
3 cloves garlic
½ cup chopped onion
2 teaspoons good-quality olive oil
¼ cup fresh lemon juice
2 tablespoons grated lemon peel
¼ cup nonfat grated Parmesan cheese
¼ cup pine nuts
1½ teaspoons dried basil
1 teaspoon dried oregano
¼ teaspoon black pepper
¼ to ½ cup vegetable stock or water

IN a bowl, cover dried tomatoes with boiling water. Let stand until tomatoes soften, about 20 minutes. Drain. In a food processor fitted with a steel blade, process softened tomatoes, garlic, and onion. Process using an off-and-on (pulsing) technique until tomatoes are puréed. Add remaining ingredients and process a few seconds until the pesto is blended. Transfer sauce to a bowl. Let stand at least 2 hours before serving to infuse flavors. Store, covered, in a bowl in the refrigerator until ready to use. Serve hot on pizza or pasta.

EACH SERVING PROVIDES:
45 calories, 36% calories from fat, 2 g fat, 0.3 g saturated fat,
0 mg cholesterol, 156 mg sodium, 3 g protein, 1 g sugar
FOOD EXCHANGES:
0.0 milk, 1.0 veg., 0.0 fruit, 0.0 bread, 0.0 meat, 0.5 fat

Penne with Warm Apple Slices and Vegetables

YIELD: 8 SERVINGS

Cooked fruit tossed with pasta is a delightful pairing for those who enjoy culinary variety.

Dressing
⅓ cup lowfat mayonnaise
⅓ cup nonfat plain yogurt
⅓ cup cider vinegar
4 cloves garlic, minced
2 teaspoons stoneground mustard
2 teaspoons dried basil

Salad
1 teaspoon reduced-fat margarine
Butter-flavored nonstick cooking spray
2 cups thinly sliced red or green cooking apples
½ teaspoon ground cinnamon
2 tablespoons brown sugar substitute
1 pound penne, pasta shells, or pasta of your choice
¾ cup thinly sliced red onion
1 cup sliced cucumber or zucchini
⅓ cup minced watercress or parsley
Salt and black pepper

IN a small bowl, mix together the mayonnaise, yogurt, and vinegar. Stir in garlic, mustard, and basil. Cover lightly and refrigerate until needed.

Heat margarine in sprayed nonstick frying pan. Sauté apple slices over medium heat until lightly brown, stirring often. Sprinkle with cinnamon and brown sugar substitute. Keep warm.

Cook pasta according to package directions and drain. In a large serving bowl, toss pasta with warm apples, onions, cucumber, and watercress. Blend in dressing, and salt and pepper to taste.

EACH SERVING PROVIDES:

295 calories, 5% calories from fat, 2 g fat, 0.3 g saturated fat,
1 mg cholesterol, 195 mg sodium, 11 g protein, 7 g sugar

FOOD EXCHANGES:

0.0 milk, 0.0 veg., 1.0 fruit, 3.0 bread, 0.0 meat, 0.0 fat

Spinach Pasta with Yellow Sun-Dried Tomato Pesto

YIELD: 6 SERVINGS

Red tomatoes can be substituted for yellow. The bright color of the pesto contrasts nicely with the spinach pasta.

½ cup Sun-Dried Tomato Pesto (see page 134),
    using yellow tomatoes
12 ounces uncooked spinach pasta
2 cups sliced yellow or red bell pepper
½ cup chopped green onions
¼ cup nonfat grated Parmesan cheese

PREPARE pesto. Set aside.
Cook pasta according to package directions, boiling just long enough to cook pasta al dente, that is, just tender. Drain and transfer to a deep bowl. Toss in pesto, peppers, green onions, and nonfat Parmesan cheese.
    Divide pasta onto 6 plates and serve immediately.

EACH SERVING PROVIDES:
222 calories, 8% calories from fat, 2.1 g fat, 0.2 g saturated fat,
0 mg cholesterol, 111 mg sodium, 12 g protein, 3 g sugar
FOOD EXCHANGES:
0.0 milk, 2.0 veg., 0.0 fruit, 2.0 bread, 0.5 meat, 0.0 fat

Thai-Style Noodles with Peanut Sauce

YIELD: 6 SERVINGS

The sophisticated flavors of this savory international dish will impress your friends and family.

1 cup nonfat plain yogurt
⅓ cup peanut butter prepared with ⅓ less fat
2 tablespoons cider vinegar
¾ teaspoon red pepper flakes, or to taste
½ teaspoon salt
6 ounces whole wheat spaghetti, thin spaghetti,
   or pasta of your choice
⅓ cup chopped cilantro
1 cup bean sprouts, washed and drained
1½ cups grated carrot
¾ cup chopped green onions

IN a small bowl, combine yogurt, peanut butter, vinegar, red pepper flakes, and salt. Mix until smooth.

Cook spaghetti according to package directions and drain. Divide pasta among 6 plates. Top with peanut sauce and sprinkle with cilantro, bean sprouts, carrots, and green onions. Serve immediately.

EACH SERVING PROVIDES:
215 calories, 24% calories from fat, 6 g fat, 2 g saturated fat,
1 mg cholesterol, 304 mg sodium, 11 g protein, 6 g sugar
FOOD EXCHANGES:
0.0 milk, 0.0 veg., 0.0 fruit, 0.0 bread, 0.0 meat, 1.0 fat

Buckwheat Noodles with Snow Peas and Asian Hot Sauce

YIELD: 6 SERVINGS

Buckwheat noodles, my favorite, are available at Asian markets and many large supermarkets.

½ pound buckwheat, soba, spinach, or other thin noodles
2 cups snow peas, trimmed and cut in half
2 cups fresh asparagus, sliced diagonally into 1-inch pieces
¾ cup chopped green onions
1 teaspoon toasted sesame seeds

Asian hot sauce
Nonstick cooking spray
1 teaspoon canola oil
¼ cup lite soy sauce
2 tablespoons red wine vinegar
2 tablespoons rice vinegar
1½ teaspoons chili–garlic paste (optional)
3 cloves garlic, minced
1 teaspoon fresh minced ginger
½ teaspoon fructose, or 1 teaspoon sugar
1 cup chopped green onions

COOK buckwheat noodles according to package directions and drain. Transfer to a serving bowl. Add snow peas and toss while noodles are still hot.

Cook asparagus in lightly salted boiling water until crisp-tender. Drain. Add asparagus to noodles. Mix in onions and sesame seeds.

In a small bowl, mix together all of the sauce ingredients. Add sauce to noodles and toss. Adjust seasonings to taste. Serve cold or at room temperature.

EACH SERVING PROVIDES:
195 calories, 10% calories from fat, 2 g fat, 0 g saturated fat,
0 mg cholesterol, 378 mg sodium, 7 g protein, 6 g sugar
FOOD EXCHANGES:
0.0 milk, 0.0 veg., 0.0 fruit, 2.5 bread, 0.0 meat, 0.5 fat

Pasta with Cabbage and Caraway Seeds

YIELD: 6 SERVINGS

Cabbage prepared with caraway seeds and pasta creates an unusual, delicious dish.

¼ cup water
2 tablespoons cider vinegar
¾ cup chopped onion
3 cups thinly sliced green cabbage, about ½ of a small head
2 cups thinly sliced red apples
½ teaspoon dried minced garlic
½ teaspoon salt
¼ teaspoon black pepper
6 ounces cholesterol-free medium noodles,
    cooked and drained
1 teaspoon caraway seeds

IN a nonstick frying pan, heat water and vinegar to boiling. Add onion, cabbage, apples, garlic, salt, and pepper. Cover and cook over medium heat for 10 minutes, stirring occasionally. Uncover and stir in drained pasta and caraway seeds. Continue cooking, stirring gently, until hot.

EACH SERVING PROVIDES:
87 calories, 3% calories from fat, 0.4 g fat, 0 g saturated fat,
0 mg cholesterol, 192 mg sodium, 2 g protein, 7 g sugar
FOOD EXCHANGES:
0.0 milk, 0.0 veg., 0.5 fruit, 1.0 bread, 0.0 meat, 0.0 fat

TOFU

TOFU

AMERICAN COOKS are becoming increasingly aware of the nutritional value and versatility of tofu. Soybean curd was developed in China many centuries ago. A practically tasteless substance, tofu gets its "glamour" from the flavors of foods and spices it's cooked with. Tofu is easily digested and is low in calories and high in protein. It is made from curdled soy milk, a product of cooked soybeans. It has a cheese-like texture and can be sliced or diced into small cubes and added to many recipes, including soups, salads, casseroles, salad dressings, and even sandwiches. Tofu is used in both sauces and desserts. It adds a meat-like texture and solidity to many dishes.

Tofu spoils easily, so it should be refrigerated and used within a week, or it can be frozen for several months. Tofu comes packed in water, which should be changed each day it's stored in the refrigerator once the package is open.

You can use tofu to supplement or replace cheese in many recipes. These recipes were prepared with extra-firm lowfat tofu.

Tofu Fajitas with Mango Barbecue Sauce

YIELD: 4 SERVINGS

Fajitas are a favorite in Southwestern cooking. Here tofu is cooked with colorful vegetables, wrapped in tortillas, and served with a tangy mango sauce.

1 cup Mango Barbecue Sauce (see page 148)
1 teaspoon canola or vegetable oil
Nonstick cooking spray
4 cloves garlic, minced
2 green bell peppers, thinly sliced
1 cup sliced onion
2 cups tomato wedges
½ cup barbecue sauce
½ teaspoon powdered cumin
4 ounces extra-firm lowfat tofu, patted dry
    and cut into ¼-inch-thick slices
4 warm 4-inch flour tortillas

P REPARE Mango Barbecue Sauce. Set aside.
Heat oil in a sprayed wok or nonstick frying pan over medium-high heat. Cook garlic, bell peppers, and onions about 3 minutes, stirring once or twice. The vegetables should be cooked through but not mushy. Add tomatoes and cook just until warm. Stir in ½ cup Mango Barbecue Sauce and cumin. Push vegetables to the side and fry the tofu slices, about 3 minutes, turning once. They will begin to brown and become crusty. Gently mix food together, allowing tofu to crumble.

Serve fajitas immediately rolled in warm flour tortillas that have been brushed on the inside with Mango Barbecue Sauce.

EACH SERVING PROVIDES:

276 calories, 17% calories from fat, 5.7 g fat, 0.6 g saturated fat,

0 mg cholesterol, 564 mg sodium, 9 g protein, 12 g sugar

FOOD EXCHANGES:

0.0 milk, 3.0 veg., 0.0 fruit, 2.0 bread, 0.0 meat, 1.0 fat

Mango Barbecue Sauce

YIELD: 18 SERVINGS (ABOUT 2½ CUPS)

Mangoes lend this sauce its sweetness while cider vinegar gives it a tang.

1 teaspoon vegetable oil
¾ cup chopped onions
3 cloves garlic, minced
6 Italian plum tomatoes, chopped, including any juice
¼ cup tomato juice
Pulp of large 1 mango
2 tablespoons cider vinegar
2 teaspoons chili sauce
½ teaspoon mustard
½ teaspoon powdered cumin

HEAT oil in nonstick saucepan over medium heat. Stir in onions and garlic. Cook and stir 5 minutes, or until onions are tender. Stir in tomatoes with liquid, tomato juice, mango pulp, cider vinegar, chili sauce, mustard, and cumin. Reduce heat to low.

Continue cooking 18 to 20 minutes, stirring occasionally. Allow to cool and purée in a blender or food processor. Place sauce in a covered container and refrigerate until needed.

EACH SERVING PROVIDES:
24 calories, 16% calories from fat, 1 g fat, 0 g saturated fat,
0 mg cholesterol, 26 mg sodium, 1 g protein, 4 g sugar
FOOD EXCHANGES:
0.0 milk, 0.0 veg., 0.0 fruit, 0.5 bread, 0.0 meat, 0.0 fat

Two-Mushroom Tofu Stir-Fry

YIELD: 6 SERVINGS

Stir-frying foods is a delicious technique for blending flavors.
Always stir-fry over medium-high heat.

1 teaspoon olive oil
Olive oil nonstick cooking spray
3 cloves garlic, minced
½ teaspoon powdered ginger
1 cup sliced leeks, white part only
2 cups sliced white mushrooms
2 cups sliced brown mushrooms
½ cup grated carrots
2 cups bean sprouts, washed and drained
¾ teaspoon dried crushed rosemary
½ teaspoon salt
¼ teaspoon black pepper
4 ounces extra-firm lowfat tofu, drained and cubed

HEAT olive oil in a sprayed wok or nonstick frying pan over
medium-high heat. Stir-fry garlic, ginger, and leeks for
about 2 minutes. Add mushrooms and carrots and stir-fry until
mushrooms are tender. Stir in bean sprouts. Season with rosemary, salt, and pepper. Add tofu and heat. Adjust seasonings
to taste.

Serve immediately over hot brown rice or couscous.

EACH SERVING PROVIDES:
73 calories, 20% calories from fat, 2 g fat, 0.2 g saturated fat,
0 mg cholesterol, 244 mg sodium, 7 g protein, 5 g sugar
FOOD EXCHANGES:
0.0 milk, 2.0 veg., 0.0 fruit, 0.0 bread, 0.5 meat, 0.0 fat

Tofu and Baby Bok Choy Stir-Fry

YIELD: 6 SERVINGS

If baby bok choy is not available, use regular bok choy in this tasty stir-fry.

½ cup vegetable stock
2 teaspoons cornstarch
2 teaspoons lite soy sauce
½ teaspoon salt
¼ teaspoon black pepper
Nonstick cooking spray
2 teaspoons vegetable oil
½ teaspoon fresh grated ginger
3 cloves garlic, minced
4 ounces extra-firm lowfat tofu, drained and diced
¾ cup chopped green onions
4 cups sliced baby bok choy
1 cup trimmed snow peas
1 cup sliced green or red bell peppers

IN a small bowl, whisk together vegetable stock, cornstarch, soy sauce, salt, and pepper. Set aside.

Spray a wok or nonstick frying pan. Heat 1 teaspoon of the oil with ginger and garlic. Cook tofu over medium heat, turning once or twice. Tofu will begin to crust. With a slotted spoon, transfer tofu to a plate.

Spray wok again and heat remaining teaspoon of oil. Stir-fry green onions for 1 to 2 minutes. Add bok choy and stir-fry until tender but not mushy. Add snow peas and bell peppers and stir-fry until hot. Return tofu to the pan and heat. Stir in vegetable stock–cornstarch mixture and cook another minute or until the sauce has thickened.

Serve with cooked brown or white rice.

NOTE: Lite soy sauce refers to soy sauce that has less sodium than regular soy sauce. It can be found in well-stocked supermarkets.

EACH SERVING PROVIDES:
75 calories, 27% calories from fat, 2.4 g fat, 0.3 g saturated fat, 0 mg cholesterol, 301 mg sodium, 6 g protein, 3 g sugar
FOOD EXCHANGES:
0.0 milk, 2.0 veg., 0.0 fruit, 0.0 bread, 0.0 meat, 0.5 fat

Couscous, Chick-Peas, and Tofu

YIELD: 6 SERVINGS

For variety, substitute cooked barley, brown rice, or white rice for the couscous.

1 teaspoon reduced-calorie margarine
Nonstick cooking spray
4 ounces extra-firm lowfat tofu, cubed
3 cups cooked couscous
4 bay leaves
¾ teaspoon dried thyme
2 teaspoons fresh lemon juice
¼ teaspoon salt
¼ teaspoon black pepper
½ cup cooked chick-peas, drained
1 tablespoon dark raisins

HEAT margarine in a sprayed nonstick frying pan over medium heat. Sauté tofu until it turns a light golden brown. Stir in couscous, bay leaves, thyme, lemon juice, salt, pepper, chick-peas, and raisins. Sauté for a few minutes, until hot. Discard bay leaves.

Serve immediately in soup bowls.

EACH SERVING PROVIDES:
156 calories, 9% calories from fat, 1.6 g fat, 0.2 g saturated fat,
0 mg cholesterol, 27 mg sodium, 9 g protein, 1 g sugar
FOOD EXCHANGES:
0.0 milk, 0.0 veg., 0.0 fruit, 2.0 bread, 0.0 meat, 0.5 fat

Tomatoes and Tofu over Orzo

YIELD: 4 SERVINGS

Orzo is a pleasant change and is easy to prepare. The tofu picks up the surrounding flavors of the vegetables and herbs.

1 teaspoon canola oil
Nonstick cooking spray
3 cloves garlic, minced
4 ounces extra-firm lowfat tofu, drained and cubed
1 cup chopped green onions
1 can (8 ounces) tomato sauce
1 cup drained chopped tomatoes
1 cup chopped red or green bell pepper
¾ teaspoon dried oregano
¾ teaspoon dried basil
¼ cup chopped fresh parsley
2 cups cooked orzo, brown rice, or pasta of your choice

HEAT oil in a sprayed nonstick frying pan over medium-high heat. Quickly sauté garlic. Add tofu and onions. Stir in remaining ingredients except cooked pasta. Continue cooking for about 5 minutes, or until mixture is hot, stirring occasionally.

Divide cooked orzo onto 4 dinner plates and spoon tofu mixture on top. Serve immediately.

EACH SERVING PROVIDES:
200 calories, 13% calories from fat, 3 g fat, 0.2 g saturated fat,
3 mg cholesterol, 370 mg sodium, 12 g protein, 4 g sugar
FOOD EXCHANGES:
0.0 milk, 2.0 veg., 0.0 fruit, 0.0 bread, 1.0 meat, 0.0 fat

Smoked Bean Curd

YIELD: 4 SERVINGS

Tofu and vegetables team up for a terrific grilled treat.

2 tablespoons lite soy sauce
¼ cup chopped green onions
½ teaspoon grated ginger
1 clove garlic, minced
1 tablespoon rice wine vinegar
½ teaspoon sesame oil (optional)
2 to 4 drops hot sauce, or to taste
4 ounces extra-firm lowfat tofu, drained
Nonstick cooking spray
8 green onions, trimmed and left whole
2 tomatoes, cut in half
½ teaspoon dried basil

IN a small bowl, whisk together soy sauce, chopped green onions, ginger, garlic, rice wine vinegar, sesame oil, and hot sauce. Cover and refrigerate until needed.

Cut drained tofu into ½-inch strips. Heat indoor grill according to manufacturer's directions. Spray top of grill with nonstick cooking spray. Place tofu and sprayed onions and tomatoes (cut side down) sprinkled with basil on the heated grill. Cover. Let tofu smoke for about 5 minutes or until done to taste. Tofu should be a golden brown color. Turn onions and tofu once with a spatula.

Arrange smoked tofu, green onions, and tomatoes decoratively on a plate and drizzle with soy sauce dressing. Serve immediately with couscous or brown rice and additional dressing on the side.

NOTE: Smoked Bean Curd can be prepared on the outdoor grill, but this recipe was tested on an indoor grill, and it worked well. When using a covered indoor grill, be sure to follow individual manufacturer's directions.

EACH SERVING PROVIDES:

60 calories, 17% calories from fat, 1.3 g fat, 0 g saturated fat, 0 mg cholesterol, 352 mg sodium, 8 g protein, 3 g sugar

FOOD EXCHANGES:

0.0 milk, 1.0 veg., 0.0 fruit, 0.0 bread, 1.0 meat, 0.0 fat

Cincinnati-Style Tofu Chili

YIELD: 8 SERVINGS

Cincinnati-Style Tofu Chili is served on a bed of pasta and topped with cheese. This is a light adaptation of what is usually a very heavy dish.

Nonstick cooking spray
4 cloves garlic, minced
1½ cup chopped onions
1 can (15 ounces) black beans, drained
2 cans (15 ounces each) kidney beans, drained
4 ounces extra-firm lowfat tofu, drained and cubed
1 can (16 ounces) crushed tomatoes, including liquid
1 tablespoon chili powder
2 teaspoons ground cumin
¼ teaspoon red pepper flakes
6 ounces thin cholesterol-free noodles, cooked according
    to package directions
2 ounces lowfat mozzarella cheese, shredded (½ cup)
1 cup chopped green onions

HEAT a sprayed large nonstick frying pan or saucepan over medium-high heat. Sauté garlic and onions until soft, stirring occasionally. If onions begin to stick, cover pan or add 2 to 3 tablespoons of vegetable stock. Mix in beans, tofu, tomatoes and liquid, chili powder, cumin, and red pepper flakes. Reduce heat to medium-low and continue cooking, stirring occasionally, for 10 minutes or until heated and liquid is mostly cooked down but chili is not dry. Stir in hot, drained noodles.

Divide chili onto 8 dinner plates or bowls. Top each serving of chili with a sprinkle of cheese and chopped green onions and serve.

EACH SERVING PROVIDES:

283 calories, 9% calories from fat, 3.2 g fat, 1 g saturated fat,

4 mg cholesterol, 698 mg sodium, 21 g protein, 3 g sugar

FOOD EXCHANGES:

0.0 milk, 1.0 veg., 0.0 fruit, 3.0 bread, 1.0 meat, 0.0 fat

MUFFINS, ROLLS, AND BREADS

••••••••••••••••

MUFFINS, ROLLS, AND BREADS

HUMANITY DOES NOT live by bread alone. Agreed! We should also have rolls and muffins. Most home-kitchen cooks allow processed, bland store-bought bread to contaminate the breakfast, lunch, and dinner table, providing nothing more than empty calories from starch. Breads should have character and be a wonderful, purposeful, and healthful addition to a meal.

In our home we bake up a continuous parade of breads, rolls, muffins, and pitas. The breads satisfy our hunger, stimulate the taste buds, and do not adversely affect the vegetarian or diabetic diet.

Blueberry Yogurt Muffins

YIELD: 12 MEDIUM OR 8 LARGE MUFFINS

If you want higher muffins, make only 8 muffins and fill each paper cup almost to the top. Dried blueberries can be substituted for fresh blueberries.

Butter-flavored nonstick cooking spray
2 cups unbleached all-purpose flour
2 tablespoons fructose, or ¼ cup sugar
2 teaspoons baking powder
½ teaspoon baking soda
½ teaspoon salt
1 cup nonfat plain yogurt
2 tablespoons canola or vegetable oil
¾ teaspoon vanilla
½ cup egg substitute, or 2 eggs
1 cup fresh blueberries or raspberries
    (if using frozen blueberries, defrost and drain)

P REHEAT oven to 400 degrees F. Line a nonstick 12-hole muffin pan with paper muffin cups. Spray paper cups or omit paper and spray the pan directly with nonstick cooking spray.

In a large mixing bowl, combine flour, fructose, baking powder, baking soda, and salt. In a small bowl, mix together yogurt, oil, vanilla, and egg substitute. Pour liquid ingredients into flour mixture and mix just until moist. Fold in blueberries. Spoon batter into muffin pan, filling cups equally.

Bake in the center of the oven for 20 minutes, or until muffins are golden brown.

EACH MEDIUM-SIZE MUFFIN PROVIDES:

110 calories, 21% calories from fat, 2.5 g fat, 0.3 g saturated fat,

0.4 mg cholesterol, 20 mg sodium, 4 g protein, 2 g sugar

FOOD EXCHANGES:

0.0 milk, 0.0 veg., 0.0 fruit, 1.0 bread, 0.0 meat, 0.5 fat

Irish Oatmeal and Currant Bannock

YIELD: 8 SERVINGS

Bannock is an oatmeal shortbread prepared in an 8-inch round pan and scored into 8 portions before baking. It is especially tasty served warm or toasted.

1¼ cups all-purpose flour
½ cup uncooked oats
2 tablespoons sugar, or 1 tablespoon fructose
¼ teaspoon salt
1 package (2¼ teaspoons) active dry yeast
½ cup nonfat milk
2 tablespoons margarine or butter
1 egg white
⅓ cup dried currants or dark raisins

IN a large bowl, combine flour, oats, sugar, salt, and yeast. In a small saucepan, heat milk and margarine until margarine melts. Add warm liquid (about 110 degrees F) to flour mixture and stir until smooth. Beat in egg white until a soft dough forms.

Cover dough with a hot, damp kitchen towel. Let sit in a warm area for 1 hour, or until dough doubles in size. Punch dough down. Stir in currants. Roll or pat dough into an 8-inch round. Place dough in a sprayed 8-inch pie plate. Score top of dough with a sharp knife into 8 equal wedges. Cover dough again and set aside in a warm area for 1 hour, or until dough has doubled in size.

Preheat oven to 375 degrees F. Bake bannock in center of oven for about 20 minutes. Bannock will be lightly golden on top and firm to the touch.

EACH SERVING PROVIDES:

155 calories, 19% calories from fat, 3.4 g fat, 0.7 g saturated fat, 0.3 mg cholesterol, 116 mg sodium, 5 g protein, 4 g sugar

FOOD EXCHANGES:

0.0 milk, 0.0 veg., 0.5 fruit, 1.5 bread, 0.0 meat, 0.5 fat

Millet Bread

YIELD: ABOUT 16 SERVINGS

Millet and whole wheat flour added to the bread make it tasty and interesting.

1 package (2¼ teaspoons) active dry yeast
1½ cups warm nonfat milk, about 110 degrees F
1 tablespoon honey
3½ cups bread flour, or as needed
½ cup stoneground whole wheat flour
¾ cup millet
¾ teaspoon salt
1 tablespoon canola oil
Nonstick cooking spray
1 egg white, lightly beaten
2 teaspoons water
1 teaspoon millet, to sprinkle on crust

IN a small bowl, combine yeast, warm milk, and honey. Let stand for about 5 minutes in a warm area until yeast begins to foam.

While yeast is proofing, mix together flours, millet, salt, and oil in a deep bowl or electric mixer with a dough attachment. Blend in yeast to form a moist (but not soggy) dough. Turn dough out onto a lightly floured board and knead 1 minute or so to smooth out dough. Place dough in a clean bowl and cover with a warm, damp kitchen towel or plastic wrap. Let stand in a draft-free area about 1 to 1½ hours, or until dough doubles in size.

Spray an 8-inch ovenproof bowl or round baking dish with nonstick cooking spray. Punch dough down with your fist and shape dough into a round. Transfer dough to sprayed dish. Cover lightly with plastic wrap and let it sit until dough doubles in size, about 1 hour.

Preheat oven to 375 degrees F. Whisk together egg white and water and brush on top of dough. Sprinkle with millet. Bake in the center of the oven for 40 minutes or until the bread tests done. It will be golden in color and make a hollow sound when tapped with finger.

Remove from bowl and cool on a wire rack.

EACH SERVING PROVIDES:
167 calories, 10% calories from fat, 2 g fat, 0.3 g saturated fat, 0.3 mg cholesterol, 114 mg sodium, 6 g protein, 3 g sugar
FOOD EXCHANGES:
0.0 milk, 0.0 veg., 0.0 fruit, 2.0 bread, 0.0 meat, 0.5 fat

Muffins, Rolls, and Breads
····

Herbed French Rolls

YIELD: 12 ROLLS

Fresh herbs add a distinct taste to these tempting rolls.

1 package (2¼ teaspoons) active dry yeast
1¼ cups warm water, about 110 degrees F
1 teaspoon sugar
3 cups bread flour
¾ teaspoon salt
¼ cup yellow or white cornmeal
1 egg white, slightly beaten
2 teaspoons water
½ cup fresh dill sprigs, flat-leaf parsley, or cilantro

IN a medium bowl, mix yeast with ¼ cup of the warm water and sugar. Let stand for about 5 minutes in a warm area until yeast foams.

Stir in remaining 1 cup of warm water, flour, and salt to form a moist dough. Knead dough using an electric mixer with a dough hook or by hand on a lightly floured cloth until dough is mixed.

Place dough in a clean bowl and cover with a warm, damp kitchen towel or plastic wrap. Put bowl in a draft-free area and let sit until dough doubles in size, about 1 hour.

Sprinkle cornmeal equally on 2 nonstick cookie sheets. Punch dough down. Divide dough into 12 equal pieces and shape them into rounds or ovals. Put rolls on prepared cookie sheet. Cover rolls lightly with aluminum foil and let sit until they double in size.

Preheat oven to 400 degrees F. Mix egg white with water and brush tops of rolls. Arrange dill decoratively on top of rolls. Press down lightly so that the fresh herbs stick to the rolls. Bake rolls in the center of the oven for 25 to 30 minutes. Rolls will be golden in color and make a hollow sound when tapped. Remove rolls from cookie sheets and allow to cool on a wire rack. Serve warm.

NOTE: To refresh rolls the second day, heat oven to 400 degrees F and warm rolls wrapped in aluminum foil for 4 to 5 minutes in the center of the oven.

EACH SERVING PROVIDES:
147 calories, 3% calories from fat, 0.5 g fat, 0.1 g saturated fat,
0 mg cholesterol, 140 mg sodium, 5 g protein, 1 g sugar
FOOD EXCHANGES:
0.0 milk, 0.0 veg., 0.0 fruit, 2.0 bread, 0.0 meat, 0.0 fat

Popovers

YIELD: 12 SERVINGS

For variety, add 2 tablespoons of grated lowfat Cheddar cheese to the batter.

Butter-flavored nonstick cooking spray
4 egg whites, at room temperature
1 cup nonfat milk
1 cup all-purpose flour
2 tablespoons canola oil

PREHEAT oven to 450 degrees F. Spray a 12-hole nonstick muffin pan.

In a food processor fitted with a steel blade or blender, process the egg whites, milk, flour, and oil for about 10 seconds.

Pour batter evenly into muffin pan. Bake popovers in the center of the oven for 20 minutes. Reduce heat to 350 degrees F. Continue baking for 18 to 20 minutes. Popovers will be golden brown. Allow to cool slightly. Run a small, sharp knife around the popovers and transfer to serving basket. They are best served hot right from the oven.

To reheat, heat oven to 350 degrees F. Put popovers on a cookie sheet and heat 15 minutes or until hot. If you have to store them, cover them tightly or wrap in aluminum foil.

EACH SERVING PROVIDES:
71 calories, 31% calories from fat, 2.5 g fat, 0.3 g saturated fat,
0.4 mg cholesterol, 29 mg sodium, 3 g protein, 1 g sugar
FOOD EXCHANGES:
0.0 milk, 0.0 veg., 0.0 fruit, 0.5 bread, 0.0 meat, 0.5 fat

Rhode Island Johnnycake

YIELD: 16 SERVINGS

A johnnycake was originally a journey cake, that is, a cake suitable to take on a long trek, in the early days of New England travel.

Butter-flavored nonstick cooking spray
1 cup unbleached all-purpose flour
1 cup yellow or white cornmeal
1 teaspoon baking soda
½ teaspoon salt
½ tablespoon fructose, or 1 tablespoon sugar
1 teaspoon dry tarragon
¼ cup egg substitute, or 1 egg
1 cup buttermilk
3 tablespoons canola oil

PREHEAT oven to 400 degrees F. Spray an 8 by 8-inch nonstick baking pan.

Sift flour, cornmeal, baking soda, salt, fructose, and tarragon in a mixing bowl. In a small bowl, mix together egg substitute and buttermilk. Stir liquid mixture into dry ingredients. Blend in oil. Stir ingredients only until they are moistened; do not overmix.

Pour batter into prepared pan. Bake in the center of the oven for 25 minutes, or until the johnnycake tests done. A tester inserted in the center of the cake will come out dry. Cut cake into 2-inch squares and serve warm.

EACH SERVING PROVIDES:
85 calories, 28% calories from fat, 3 g fat, 0.3 g saturated fat,
1 mg cholesterol, 170 mg sodium, 3 g protein, 1 g sugar
FOOD EXCHANGES:
0.0 milk, 0.0 veg., 0.0 fruit, 1.0 bread, 0.0 meat, 0.5 fat

Muffins, Rolls, and Breads
····

Buttermilk Rolls

YIELD: 22 SMALL ROLLS

Buttermilk is the secret for making these light, rich rolls.

1 package (2¼ teaspoons) active dry yeast
¼ cup warm water, about 110 degrees F
1 tablespoon plus 1 teaspoon sugar
3 cups unbleached all-purpose flour
½ teaspoon baking soda
¾ cup buttermilk, at room temperature
¾ teaspoon salt
3 tablespoons margarine, softened
Butter-flavored nonstick cooking spray
1 egg white, slightly beaten
1 teaspoon poppy seeds

IN a medium bowl, mix yeast with warm water and 1 teaspoon sugar. Let stand for about 5 minutes in a warm area until yeast foams.

Stir in flour, baking soda, salt, and buttermilk. Mix in softened margarine to form a soft dough. Knead dough using an electric mixer with a dough hook or by hand on a lightly floured cloth until dough is mixed.

Place dough in a clean bowl and cover with a warm, damp kitchen towel or plastic wrap. Put bowl in a draft-free area and let dough rise until it doubles in size, about 1 hour.

Punch dough down. Knead for 2 to 3 minutes more. Shape dough into walnut-size balls and set in a sprayed miniature muffin pan. Cover lightly and let dough rise until it doubles in size, 35 to 40 minutes.

Preheat oven to 375 degrees F. Using a pastry brush, brush top of bread with lightly beaten egg white. Sprinkle with poppy seeds. Bake rolls in the center of the oven for 25 minutes, or until rolls are a golden brown and make a hollow sound when tapped. Remove from pan and allow to cool on a wire rack.

EACH ROLL PROVIDES:

76 calories, 13% calories from fat, 2 g fat, 0.3 g saturated fat, 0.4 mg cholesterol, 130 mg sodium, 2.4 g protein, 2 g sugar

FOOD EXCHANGES:

0.0 milk, 0.0 veg., 0.0 fruit, 1.0 bread, 0.0 meat, 0.0 fat

Oregano Whole Wheat Pita Bread

YIELD: 12 PITA BREADS

For a special taste treat, use Greek mountain-grown oregano if you can find it.

1 package (2¼ teaspoons) active dry yeast
1 teaspoon sugar
1 cup warm water, about 110 degrees F
2 cups bread flour
¾ cup plus 2 tablespoons stoneground whole wheat flour
3 tablespoons dried oregano
¾ teaspoon salt
1 tablespoon canola oil or good-quality olive oil

IN a small bowl, stir yeast and sugar into warm water. Set bowl in a warm area and let stand until yeast begins to bubble, about 5 minutes.

In a large bowl, mix together flours, oregano, salt, and oil. Stir in yeast mixture. Mix 2 to 3 minutes with an electric mixer fitted with a dough hook or by hand with a wooden spoon.

Knead dough on a lightly floured pastry cloth until it reaches a smooth, medium consistency. Put dough in a bowl and cover with a warm, damp towel or plastic wrap. Let dough rise in a warm area until it has doubled in size, 1 to 1½ hours. Punch dough down. Allow it to rise for another 35 minutes.

Divide dough into 12 equal pieces. Roll each piece into 4-inch rounds. Cover pita rounds lightly with aluminum foil or plastic wrap and let rise for 30 minutes.

Preheat oven to 500 degrees F. Heat a large, ungreased non-stick baking sheet in the oven for 8 to 10 minutes.

Using pot holders to remove hot pan, arrange bread rounds 1 inch apart on the baking sheet. Bake immediately on the lowest oven rack for 5 minutes. Bread rounds will puff up and turn light brown. Serve immediately.

NOTE: To reheat, heat pita bread in a 250-degree oven for 12 to 15 minutes. Store covered in aluminum foil.

EACH SERVING PROVIDES:
126 calories, 11% calories from fat, 1.7 g fat, 0.2 g saturated fat,
0 mg cholesterol, 135 mg sodium, 5 g protein, 1 g sugar
FOOD EXCHANGES:
0.0 milk, 0.0 veg., 0.0 fruit, 2.0 bread, 0.0 meat, 0.0 fat

Rosemary Cornmeal Monkey Bread

YIELD: 16 SERVINGS (1 LOAF)

Monkey bread is a "pull-apart" bread that's as delicious as it is fun to eat.

1 package (2¼ teaspoons) active dry yeast
1 teaspoon sugar
1 cup plus 2 tablespoons warm water, about 110 degrees F
1 tablespoon reduced-calorie margarine, softened
¾ teaspoon salt
⅓ cup nonfat powdered milk
¾ cup yellow or white cornmeal
2 tablespoons crumbled dried rosemary
2½ to 3 cups unbleached all-purpose flour
Butter-flavored nonstick cooking spray

IN a bowl, stir yeast and sugar into warm water. Let stand for about 5 minutes in a warm area until yeast foams. Add margarine.

While yeast is proofing, mix together salt, powdered milk, cornmeal, crumbled rosemary, and flour in a deep bowl or in an electric mixer with a dough hook. Add yeast mixture and mix. Dough will be soft and very pliable. Turn dough out onto a lightly floured board. Knead 2 to 3 minutes more to smooth out dough.

Place dough in a clean bowl and cover with a warm, damp cloth or plastic wrap. Put bowl in a draft-free area and let dough rise until it doubles in size, 1 to 1½ hours. Punch dough down.

Divide dough into 16 equal pieces and shape them into balls. Spray an 8-inch baking pan and arrange dough balls in two layers in the prepared pan. Cover and let rise for 1 hour. Preheat oven to 350 degrees F. Bake bread in center of oven for 30 minutes. Bread will be golden brown and make a hollow sound when tapped. Allow to cool in pan for 5 minutes and transfer to a wire rack to continue cooling.

EACH SERVING PROVIDES:

103 calories, 7% calories from fat, 0.9 g fat, 0.2 g saturated fat, 0.3 mg cholesterol, 116 mg sodium, 4 g protein, 1 g sugar

FOOD EXCHANGES:

0.0 milk, 0.0 veg., 0.0 fruit, 1.5 bread, 0.0 meat, 0.0 fat

DESSERTS

• • • • • • • • • • • • • • •

• • • • • • • • • • • • • •

DESSERTS

MY HUSBAND JERRY always says the only reason he eats his meal is to get to dessert. I have been delighted by his reaction to this chapter as he has periodically passed through my kitchen during this book's development and sampled my progress. While I tested recipes, my kitchen often took on the incredibly seductive atmosphere of a pastry shop, ice cream parlor, and candy store. My work paid off: The desserts in this chapter are as healthful and diabetic-safe as they are scrumptious.

Many of these lowfat recipes could not have been developed as recently as ten years ago, before the availability of lowfat and nonfat yogurt and other diet-smart ingredients. In addition, it's now routine for cooks to substitute cocoa for higher fat chocolate in recipes. These handy ingredients make it easy to create delectable chocolate desserts that diabetics can enjoy.

Chocolate French Toast with Chocolate Drizzle

YIELD: 4 SERVINGS

French toast flavored with cocoa and drizzled with chocolate sauce goes from the breakfast table to a fine-dining dessert.

Chocolate Drizzle (optional; see page 183)
1 cup egg substitute, or 4 eggs
1 cup nonfat milk
2 tablespoons unsweetened Dutch cocoa
1 tablespoon fructose, or 2 tablespoons sugar
4 slices French bread or cholesterol-free white bread,
   ½ inch thick
1½ tablespoons reduced-fat margarine
Butter-flavored nonstick cooking spray

PREPARE Chocolate Drizzle, if using, and set aside. In a shallow bowl, mix together egg substitute, milk, cocoa, and fructose. Dip and soak each bread slice on both sides in the chocolate mixture. In a sprayed nonstick frying pan, melt margarine over medium heat.

Cook the dipped bread until lightly browned on both sides, about 2 to 3 minutes per side. Cut slices of bread in half and serve drizzled with Chocolate Drizzle or sprinkled very lightly with confectioners' sugar.

EACH SERVING PROVIDES:
177 calories, 10% calories from fat, 3.7 g fat, 0.8 g saturated fat,
1.0 mg cholesterol, 340 mg sodium, 11 g protein, 3 g sugar
FOOD EXCHANGES:
0.0 milk, 0.0 veg., 0.0 fruit, 1.5 bread, 1.0 meat, 0.0 fat

Chocolate Drizzle

YIELD: 6 SERVINGS OF 2 TABLESPOONS EACH (¾ CUP)

This rich sauce is a fantastic accompaniment to many desserts.

3 tablespoons unsweetened cocoa
1 tablespoon cornstarch
2 teaspoons fructose, or 4 teaspoons sugar
½ cup plus 2 tablespoons water
1 teaspoon vanilla extract
3 packets (0.035 ounce each) granulated sugar substitute

IN a small, heavy saucepan, mix together cocoa, cornstarch, and fructose. Whisk in water. Bring mixture to a boil over medium heat, whisking almost constantly. Reduce heat to medium and cook for 30 seconds to 1 minute more, or until mixture thickens to desired consistency. Remove from heat. Stir in vanilla and sugar substitute. Adjust sweetness to taste.

Allow sauce to cool. Store covered in the refrigerator. Reheat to serve.

EACH SERVING PROVIDES:
18 calories, 11% calories from fat, 0.3 g fat, 0 g saturated fat,
0 mg cholesterol, 1.8 mg sodium, 1 g protein, 0 g sugar
FOOD EXCHANGES:
0.0 milk, 0.0 veg., 0.0 fruit, 0.0 bread, 0.0 meat, 0.0 fat

Chocolate Crepes with Tropical Fruit

YIELD: 12 SERVINGS

Chocolate crepes are the foundation of many tempting desserts. You can fill crepes with a portion of prepared, set, sugar-free chocolate or pistachio pudding and top with a dollop of defrosted nondairy topping—for just one mouthwatering example. Or try filling crepes with nonfat frozen yogurt and drizzling them with chocolate or coffee sauce.

Crepes
¾ cup egg substitute, or 3 eggs
1 cup unbleached all-purpose flour
1 tablespoon fructose, or 2 tablespoons sugar
2 tablespoons Dutch cocoa
1¼ cups buttermilk
⅔ cup water, or as necessary to make batter smooth
1 teaspoon reduced-calorie margarine, melted
Butter-flavored nonstick cooking spray

Tropical fruit
½ cup sliced banana
1 tablespoon fresh lime juice
2 mangos, peeled, seeded, and chopped (about 2 cups fruit)
1 cup chopped fresh pineapple
1 cup peeled, seeded, chopped papaya
1 star fruit, sliced, for garnish (optional)

IN a mixing bowl or blender, combine egg substitute, flour, fructose, cocoa, buttermilk, water, and margarine. Before using batter, let it stand, covered, for 20 minutes. Stir batter before cooking.

Heat a nonstick crepe pan over medium-high heat and spray with nonstick cooking spray. It is only necessary to spray pan for the first and second crepes, unless they begin to stick. Use a ¼ cup measuring cup to measure and pour each crepe. Lift and tilt the pan to evenly distribute batter, working quickly. Cook crepe until bottom is golden brown. Turn and cook only a few seconds more, until set. Remove from pan, allow to cool, and stack with a sheet of aluminum foil separating each crepe. Repeat until all of the batter is used. Add water by the tablespoon if batter becomes too thick. Fill crepes immediately or cover and refrigerate for later use. Crepes can be prepared up to a day before serving. Cover each one individually with a sheet of foil and wrap tightly. Refrigerate until ready to use.

Combine all remaining ingredients except sliced star fruit. To serve, line a footed glass with 1 warm crepe. Spoon in about ⅓ cup tropical fruit mixture and top with a star fruit. Or roll crepes in the traditional style with the fruit in the middle.

EACH SERVING PROVIDES:
80 calories, 7% calories from fat, 1 g fat, 0.2 g saturated fat,
1 mg cholesterol, 44 mg sodium, 3 g protein, 8 g sugar
FOOD EXCHANGES:
0.0 milk, 0.0 veg., 1.0 fruit, 0.5 bread, 0.0 meat, 0.0 fat

Apple–Raisin Multigrain Bread Pudding

YIELD: 6 SERVINGS

Bread pudding is comfort food at its best, conjuring up favorite memories. To measure sliced bread, tear it into ½-inch pieces and pack in a measuring cup.

2 cups day-old sliced multigrain bread
2 cups nonfat milk
1 cup chopped, peeled apple, such as Granny Smith
2 tablespoons dark raisins
1 egg
2 egg whites
¼ teaspoon salt
1¼ teaspoons vanilla extract
Sugar substitute equal to 4 teaspoons sugar

P UT bread pieces in a 2-quart ovenproof bowl. Pour milk over bread. Using a fork, push bread down into the milk so the bread is covered with milk. Let stand for 20 minutes. Stir once or twice.

Preheat oven to 375 degrees F.

Mix apples and raisins with bread and milk. In a separate bowl, mix together egg, egg whites, salt, vanilla extract, and sugar substitute. Stir egg mixture into bread mixture.

Set ovenproof bowl in a larger pan and place in the center of the oven. Pour hot water halfway up sides of outer pan. Bake for 1 hour, or until a knife inserted in the center of pudding comes out clean. Serve warm.

EACH SERVING PROVIDES:

99 calories, 13% calories from fat, 1.5 g fat, 0.5 g saturated fat, 37 mg cholesterol, 207 mg sodium, 7 g protein, 9 g sugar

FOOD EXCHANGES:

0.0 milk, 0.0 veg., 0.5 fruit, 0.5 bread, 0.5 meat, 0.0 fat

Poached Pears

YIELD: 6 SERVINGS

Poached Pears are tender, gently cooked pears flavored with cinnamon sticks and a pinch of rosemary. This elegant dessert is good plain or with Chocolate Drizzle.

6 cups water
1 tablespoon lime juice
2 cinnamon sticks
¼ teaspoon grated nutmeg
2 bay leaves
Pinch of rosemary
6 small ripe pears

POUR water into a small saucepan. Mix in lime juice, cinnamon sticks, nutmeg, bay leaves, and rosemary. Bring mixture to a boil over medium heat. Reduce heat to medium-low.

While liquid is heating, peel pears, leaving stems intact. Add pears to simmering spiced water, cover, and continue cooking for 10 to 12 minutes. Pears should be tender when pierced with the tip of a knife. Remove pears from syrup with a slotted spoon and allow to cool.

Serve pears at room temperature, plain or with Chocolate Drizzle (see page 183).

EACH SERVING PROVIDES:
100 calories, 6% calories from fat, 0.7 g fat, 0 g saturated fat,
0 mg cholesterol, 0 mg sodium, 1 g protein, 17 g sugar
FOOD EXCHANGES:
0.0 milk, 0.0 veg., 1.5 fruit, 0.0 bread, 0.0 meat, 0.0 fat

Brown Rice and Currant Custard Pudding

YIELD: 8 SERVINGS

You can use brown or white rice in this recipe, but the brown rice gives the pudding a slight nutty taste. This is good served warm or at room temperature.

Butter-flavored nonstick cooking spray
3 cups cooked brown rice
4 cups nonfat milk
¼ cup sugar, or 2 tablespoons fructose
3 egg whites, beaten until soft peaks form
¼ cup currants (optional)
1 teaspoon vanilla extract
½ teaspoon cinnamon

PREHEAT oven to 350 degrees F. Spray a 3-quart bowl-shaped baking dish. In a mixing bowl, stir together rice, milk, fructose, egg whites, currants, vanilla, and cinnamon. Pour mixture into prepared dish. Bake about 1 hour and 20 minutes, uncovered, or until the pudding is set. Allow to cool in oven with door open.

Serve warm in shallow dessert dishes topped with a dollop of defrosted fat-free nondairy whipped topping.

EACH SERVING PROVIDES:
157 calories, 5% calories from fat, 0.9 g fat, 0.3 g saturated fat, 2.0 mg cholesterol, 88 mg sodium, 8 g protein, 12 g sugar
FOOD EXCHANGES:
0.5 milk, 0.0 veg., 0.0 fruit, 1.5 bread, 0.0 meat, 0.0 fat

Pear Grunt

YIELD: 8 SERVINGS

The origin of the name of this fruit dumpling dish is lost in culinary history, but the rumor is that the noise the dessert makes as it cooks sounds like "grunt."

¾ cup unbleached all-purpose flour
2 tablespoons fructose, or 4 tablespoons sugar
1 teaspoon baking powder
¼ teaspoon salt
3 tablespoons margarine
3 tablespoons nonfat milk
4 cups ripe but firm peeled, sliced pears
¼ cup dried cranberries
¼ cup freshly squeezed orange juice
½ cup water
½ teaspoon ground cinnamon
⅛ teaspoon ground nutmeg
⅛ teaspoon ground cloves

IN a small bowl or a food processor fitted with a steel blade, mix together flour, 1 tablespoon fructose, baking powder, salt, and margarine. Blend in milk to form a soft dough. Set aside.

In a medium saucepan, stir together the pear slices, cranberries, remaining tablespoon of fructose, orange juice, water, and spices. Bring fruit mixture to a boil over medium heat. Reduce heat to medium-low and cook for 5 minutes more, stirring often. While fruit is cooking, drop dough by the tablespoonful onto fruit. Cook, uncovered, for 5 minutes. Cover and cook 8 to 10 minutes, until dumpling batter is cooked.

Spoon cooked fruit with a dumpling on top into a dessert dish. Top with defrosted fat-free nondairy whipped topping, if desired, and serve immediately.

EACH SERVING PROVIDES:

184 calories, 23% calories from fat, 4.9 g fat, 0.9 g saturated fat,

0 mg cholesterol, 161 mg sodium, 2 g protein, 19 g sugar

FOOD EXCHANGES:

0.0 milk, 0.0 veg., 2.0 fruit, 0.0 bread, 0.0 meat, 1.0 fat

Individual Apricot Noodle Puddings

YIELD: 12 SERVINGS

This is a dessert, a nutritious breakfast, a snack, or a side dish. Raisins or currants can be substituted for apricots.

Butter-flavored nonstick cooking spray
1 cup nonfat cottage cheese
¾ cup nonfat milk
¼ cup fructose, or ½ cup sugar
½ cup egg substitute, or 2 eggs
⅓ cup oat bran cereal flakes or other cereal of your choice
½ teaspoon salt
1 teaspoon vanilla extract
6 ounces cholesterol-free thin noodles, cooked according
    to package directions, drained, and cooled
6 ounces dried apricots, cut into thin strips

PREHEAT oven to 325 degrees F. Spray a 12-hole nonstick muffin pan with cooking spray.

In a large bowl, combine cottage cheese, milk, fructose, egg substitute, oat bran cereal, salt, and vanilla. Stir in drained noodles and apricots. Divide mixture evenly into prepared muffin cups. Place pan in the center of the oven. Bake until puddings are cooked, about 30 minutes. To test, insert a knife in center; it will come out clean when pudding is done. Cool slightly.

To loosen puddings, run a knife around edges while they are still warm. Force them out of the pan with a spoon.

Puddings can be frozen and reheated in the microwave. Best served warm.

EACH SERVING PROVIDES:

124 calories, 2% calories from fat, 0.3 g fat, 0 g saturated fat, 0 mg cholesterol, 166 mg sodium, 6 g protein, 7 g sugar

FOOD EXCHANGES:

0.0 milk, 0.0 veg., 0.5 fruit, 0.5 bread, 1.0 meat, 0.0 fat

Stewed Fruit

YIELD: 8 SERVINGS

One of my early food memories is the magic my mother would make with soft fruit. When the bowl of summer fruit was beginning to turn soft, she would peel, slice, and stew complementary fruits. With different fruit in season, the recipe was never the same twice. When you try this recipe, vary the fruits according to whatever is left in your fruit bowl.

6 ripe pears
2 ripe apples
½ cup blueberries, fresh or frozen
3 tablespoons freshly squeezed orange juice
¼ teaspoon ground cinnamon
1 tablespoon fructose, or sugar substitute equivalent to
   1 tablespoon sugar

PEEL and slice pears and apples. In a medium saucepan, mix together pears, apples, blueberries, orange juice, and cinnamon. Bring fruit mixture to a boil over medium heat. Reduce heat to medium-low and cook for 15 minutes, stirring once or twice. Taste to adjust seasonings. Allow stewed fruit to cool and stir in fructose.

Pour fruit into a serving bowl and serve warm or cold. Store fruit covered in the refrigerator.

EACH SERVING PROVIDES:
104 calories, 5% calories from fat, 0 g fat, 0 g saturated fat,
0 mg cholesterol, 1 mg sodium, 1 g protein, 18 g sugar
FOOD EXCHANGES:
0.0 milk, 0.0 veg., 1.5 fruit, 0.0 bread, 0.0 meat, 0.0 fat

Tangerine Custard Sauce with Sliced Fruit

YIELD: 4 SERVINGS

Tangerine is a refreshing flavor that blends well with the vanilla custard and sliced fruit.

1 package (1 ounce) sugar-free instant vanilla pudding mix
2 cups nonfat milk
2 tablespoons grated tangerine or orange peel
3 tablespoons fresh tangerine juice, orange juice,
    or dry white wine
2 cups sliced apples, skin left on
1 cup sliced pears, bananas, or peeled tangerines
½ cup raspberries or blueberries (optional)

IN a medium bowl, add pudding mix and stir in milk, tangerine peel, and juice. Beat for 2 minutes. Let mixture stand at room temperature for 5 minutes. Stir again and pool sauce onto 6 chilled dessert plates. Arrange cut fruit decoratively on top of sauce and serve.

EACH SERVING PROVIDES:
119 calories, 4% calories from fat, 0.5 g fat, 0.2 g saturated fat,
1.5 mg cholesterol, 51 mg sodium, 3.5 g protein, 14 g sugar
FOOD EXCHANGES:
0.5 milk, 0.0 veg., 1.0 fruit, 0.0 bread, 0.0 meat, 0.0 fat

Key Lime Chiffon Pie

YIELD: 8 SERVINGS

Many thanks to my friend Joanna Gutmann for her help test-
ing this classic recipe.

1 Graham Cracker Crust (see page 198)
4 cups nonfat Key lime yogurt with aspartame and fructose,
    drain any liquid
1½ tablespoons grated lime peel
1½ cups defrosted fat-free whipped topping
1 lime, sliced thin, for garnish

PREPARE crust and refrigerate it for 20 minutes or longer.
In a deep bowl, mix together yogurt, lime peel, and whipped
topping. Mound the filling into the crust. Cover pie lightly with
aluminum foil. Freeze pie for 2 hours, or until firm.

Set pie on counter at room temperature for about 1 hour
before serving, so pie softens slightly but does not defrost
completely. Slice pie, set on dessert dishes, and garnish with
lime slices.

EACH SERVING PROVIDES:
116 calories, 29% calories from fat, 4 g fat, 2.7 g saturated fat,
0 mg cholesterol, 114 mg sodium, 5 g protein, 6 g sugar
FOOD EXCHANGES:
0.0 milk, 0.0 veg., 0.0 fruit, 1.0 bread, 0.0 meat, 1.0 fat

Blueberry Pie

Blueberry pie is a traditional summertime treat, but you can use frozen blueberries to enjoy this pie any time.

1 (9-inch) Amaranth Graham Cracker Crust (see page 199)
2 packages (0.3 ounces each) sugar-free raspberry gelatin
2 cups boiling water
½ cup cold water
2 cups nonfat blended blueberry yogurt with aspartame
2 cups fresh or defrosted, drained blueberries

PREPARE crust and chill for at least 20 minutes. Pour gelatin in a mixing bowl. Stir in boiling water and stir until smooth. Blend in cold water and allow gelatin mixture to cool to room temperature. Stir in yogurt.

Refrigerate filling until almost set, about 1 hour. Mix in blueberries. Mound filling into prepared pie crust.

Refrigerate pie 2 to 3 hours, or until firm. Slice and serve on dessert plates.

EACH SERVING PROVIDES:
190 calories, 11% calories from fat, 2.1 g fat, 0.4 g saturated fat,
0 mg cholesterol, 444 mg sodium, 10 g protein, 16 g sugar
FOOD EXCHANGES:
0.5 milk, 0.0 veg., 1.0 fruit, 1.0 bread, 0.0 meat, 0.0 fat

Graham Cracker Crust

YIELD: 1 (9-INCH) PIE CRUST (6 TO 8 SERVINGS)

Use plain, cinnamon, or chocolate graham crackers in this
quick and easy pie crust.

7 reduced-fat graham crackers
½ teaspoon ground cinnamon
1 tablespoon reduced-calorie margarine, softened

CRUMBLE graham crackers into a food processor. Pulse a few
seconds until crumbs form. Or, place the graham crackers
between two sheets of waxed paper and crush with a rolling pin.
Transfer crumbs to a bowl and mix in margarine and cinnamon.

Pat crumb mixture into bottom and up the sides of a 9-inch
pie plate. Chill crust until ready to use.

EACH SERVING PROVIDES:
32 calories, 20% calories from fat, 0.8 g fat, 0.2 g saturated fat,
0 mg cholesterol, 41 mg sodium, 1 g protein, 0 g sugar
FOOD EXCHANGES:
0.0 milk, 0.0 veg., 0.0 fruit, 0.5 bread, 0.0 meat, 0.0 fat

Amaranth Graham Cracker Crust

YIELD: 1 (9-INCH) PIE CRUST (6 TO 8 SERVINGS)

Amaranth is an old grain that is finding new popularity. If amaranth flakes aren't available, use 5 regular graham crackers.

7 reduced-fat cinnamon graham crackers
1 cup amaranth cereal flakes
¼ teaspoon ground nutmeg
1 tablespoon reduced-calorie margarine, softened

IN a food processor, process graham crackers along with amaranth cereal flakes, nutmeg, and margarine. Pulse for a few seconds until crumbs form. Or, place the crackers and cereal between two sheets of waxed paper and crush with a rolling pin. In a bowl, combine crumbs with nutmeg and margarine.

Pat crumb mixture into the bottom (and up the sides, if desired) of a 9-inch pie pan. Chill crust until ready to use.

EACH SERVING PROVIDES:
59 calories, 29% calories from fat, 2 g fat, 0.4 g saturated fat,
0 mg cholesterol, 72 mg sodium, 2 g protein, 0 g sugar
FOOD EXCHANGES:
0.0 milk, 0.0 veg., 0.0 fruit, 0.5 bread, 0.0 meat, 0.5 fat

Espresso Gelatin

YIELD: 4 SERVINGS

Coffee is the flavor of the moment, so here it is used in a sophisticated gelatin dessert.

4 teaspoons unflavored gelatin
2 cups cold water
1 tablespoon fructose, or 2 tablespoons sugar
1 cinnamon stick
2 teaspoons grated orange peel
2 tablespoons instant powdered espresso, or to taste
½ cup defrosted fat-free nondairy whipped topping (optional)

IN a saucepan, stir together the gelatin and the cold water over medium heat. Let gelatin soften, about 5 minutes, stirring once or twice. Stir in the fructose, cinnamon stick, orange peel, and instant espresso. Simmer until gelatin dissolves, about 5 minutes. Discard cinnamon stick. Pour gelatin into four ½-cup individual molds.

Refrigerate molds until gelatin is firm, 1½ to 2 hours. To unmold, loosen the gelatin mold by dipping each mold in hot water, just up to the rim, for a few seconds. Unmold onto individual dessert plates. Serve plain, with Coffee Sauce (see page 201), or spoon whipped topping on the side.

EACH SERVING PROVIDES:
49 calories, 30% calories from fat, 2 g fat, 1.6 g saturated fat,
0 mg cholesterol, 7 mg sodium, 3 g protein, 1 g sugar
FOOD EXCHANGES:
0.0 milk, 0.0 veg., 0.0 fruit, 0.0 bread, 0.0 meat, 0.5 fat

Coffee Sauce

YIELD: 8 SERVINGS (ABOUT 2 TABLESPOONS EACH)

Serve this decadant sauce with Espresso Gelatin (page 200).

2 teaspoons cornstarch
1 cup nonfat milk
¼ cup Dutch or regular cocoa
1 teaspoon instant powdered espresso
1 teaspoon vanilla extract
¼ teaspoon ground cinnamon
2 teaspoons fructose or 4 teaspoons sugar

IN a small saucepan, whisk together cornstarch and milk. Whisk in cocoa and instant espresso. Bring mixture to a boil. Reduce heat to low and continue cooking for 5 minutes, stirring occasionally. Sauce will begin to thicken.

Remove pan from heat. Stir in vanilla, cinnamon, and fructose. Allow to cool slightly before serving. To store, allow to cool completely, pour sauce into a covered container, and refrigerate.

EACH SERVING PROVIDES:
24 calories, 10% calories from fat, 0.4 g fat, 0.1 g saturated fat,
0.5 mg cholesterol, 18 mg sodium, 1.6 g protein, 2 g sugar
FOOD EXCHANGES:
0.0 milk, 0.0 veg., 0.0 fruit, 0.0 bread, 0.0 meat, 0.0 fat

Cappuccino Yogurt Drink

YIELD: 4 SERVINGS

This refreshing drink combines the flavors of rich coffee and cinnamon.

1 cup sliced ripe banana
2 cups nonfat milk
2 cups nonfat coffee yogurt
½ teaspoon instant coffee
⅛ teaspoon ground cinnamon
⅛ teaspoon ground nutmeg

IN a blender or a food processor, combine all ingredients and process a few seconds until smooth.

Pour into a container, cover, and refrigerate until cold. Divide into 4 chilled footed glasses. Sprinkle with extra cinnamon or add a cinnamon stick to each drink, for garnish.

EACH SERVING PROVIDES:
143 calories, 3% calories from fat, 0.5 g fat, 0.3 g saturated fat,
2.0 mg cholesterol, 134 mg sodium, 9 g protein, 18 g sugar
FOOD EXCHANGES:
1.0 milk, 0.0 veg., 1.0 fruit, 0.0 bread, 0.0 meat, 0.0 fat

INDEX

●●●●●●●●●●●●●●●●●●●●

····

Index
····
204

Index
••••
205

Index
••••
207

Index
····
208

Index
••••
209

Index
••••
211

Index
••••